T H E   B O O K   O F

Quiches and Savory Pies

THE BOOK OF

Quiches and Savory Pies

MANDY PHIPPS

HPBooks

ANOTHER BEST SELLING VOLUME FROM HPBOOKS

HPBooks
Published by the Berkley Publishing Group
A division of Penguin Group (USA) Inc.
375 Hudson Street
New York, NY 10014

Copyright © Salamander Books, 2005
By arrangement with Salamander Books

An imprint of **Chrysalis** Books Group plc

Editor: Katherine Edelston
Designer: Cara Hamilton
Production: Don Campaniello
Filmset and reproduction by: Anorax Imaging Ltd

Notice: The information contained in this book is true and
complete to the best of our knowledge. All recommendations
are made without any guarantees on the part of the author or
the publisher. The author and publisher disclaim all liability
in connection with the use of this information.

Visit our website at www.penguin.com

ISBN 1-55788-452-8

Printed and bound in Spain

10 9 8 7 6 5 4 3 2 1

ACKNOWLEDGMENTS:

This book is dedicated to my late father, John Charles
Phipps—who always enjoyed a taste of homemade cooking.

I would like to thank Lesley Wilson and Katherine Edelston
for their hard work and patience over my deliberations and
to all those at Salamander Books who have worked tirelessly
in the production of this book. Also Phil Wilkins,
photographer, and Carol Tennant, part-stylist, for their
efforts in getting the recipes "captured."

Finally a big thank-you to my family for "releasing" me to
the hard days and long nights it has taken to make this
book happen.

CONTENTS

INTRODUCTION

Serving up a homemade pie to a table of eager diners is a very satisfying experience. Hot, flaky, melt-in-the-mouth pastry encasing a richly flavored filling is truly enjoyable "comfort food"—both to prepare and to eat. Making pastry, like many things in life, improves with practice and although there are convenient ready-made chilled and frozen pastries available to buy they really don't compare with pastry that has been made at home. The recipes in this book have been created to appeal to both the novice pastry cook and the experienced "master."

TIPS FOR SUCCESSFUL PASTRY MAKING

Filling Ingredients: this particularly applies to quiches, tarts, and any recipes involving a pie crust.

Foods such as onions, mushrooms, zucchini, eggplant, bacon, and ground beef have either a high water or fat content and are best pre-cooked and drained on paper towel before placing in the pie crust. This helps prevent the pastry becoming soggy.

Below: A food processor can make preparation much easier but be careful not to overheat the dough.

Egg Wash: some cooks favor the use of egg or milk to glaze their pastries. Egg alone, if not well beaten, can be difficult to brush as well as producing too much of a golden finish. Too much milk can result in a pale appearance and soggy texture. In this book a blend of milk and egg (1 x large egg, beaten plus 1/4 cup milk, blended together) has been used. This mixture provides an easy-to-use texture and an even golden-brown finish. Remember to make sure that the brush used is specifically for dough and not for oil, as it will not glide over the pastry well.

Use of Salt: the increased use of salt has been linked to high blood pressure and subsequent strain on the heart. Many processed foods have high levels of "hidden salt" and for this reason additional salt, by way of seasoning, has not been used here. Ingredients such as butter, hard and soft cheese, cured bacon, salami, and tomato sauces all have added salt. If, on tasting, the cook feels that more salt is needed then naturally that is down to personal preference.

Utensils: apart from the common sense items such as mixing bowls, measuring spoons and cups, and

weighing scales it is important to mention the advantages of using a food processor to make dough.

Dough benefits most from minimal handling and being kept cool prior to cooking. The traditional "cutting in" method can sometimes lead to over-handling and therefore melting of the butter. This in turn results in a sticky mixture, which is difficult to work with. If more flour is added to try and overcome the problem then the balance of ingredients is upset and an over-dry dough is created. This in turn becomes difficult to roll out and will not bake well.

Using a processor reduces handling and butter, herbs, and other added ingredients used to flavor the dough are blended in quickly and evenly. Over use of a food processor can still overheat the dough but this can be avoided by using the dough blade attachment and blending on a pulse setting. It is still important to chill the dough prior to rolling out and if over-processed during the addition of the egg yolk/water/milk stage it will need to be chilled for longer.

Which sort of container is best to cook pie dough in? The use of a metal pan or plate is by far the best choice when looking to bake dough well. It is the best conductor of heat and will therefore help to crisp and cook the pie dough more efficiently than ceramic or glass alternatives.

Baking Blind—is it really necessary? This is the process of baking a pie

Above: There are a wide variety of rolling and cutting utensils that you can use—here are some of the basics.

crust either partially or completely prior to adding the filling ingredients with the main intention of preventing a soggy, uncooked pie crust. This is particularly good for pies or quiches with a heavier type of filling such as ground beef and rice or a lot of vegetables; both of which have a higher water and density content than the traditional egg and herb filling and are therefore more likely to hinder the cooking of the pie crust.

Some multi-function oven manufacturers claim that there is no need for baking dough blind when using a particular oven setting but this is very variable, dependent on a number of different factors including the type of pie dough, filling, and cooking container, and the depth of the pie or quiche and so on.

How to bake blind
Method 1: after rolling, lining, and trimming the dough to fit the pan or dish, crumple a piece of waxed paper, larger than the pie dough itself, and lay it on top of the dough. Fill with ceramic pie weights or any uncooked rice or pulses and bake in a hot oven, usually 400F (200C), for 10 minutes (see Fig.1). Remove the paper and beans and return to the oven for another 5–10 minutes.

NB. After removing the paper and weights the pie crust can be brushed

Fig.1

Fig.2

with lightly beaten egg white or a little egg yolk or egg wash before being returned to the oven. This creates a "seal" against the filling ingredients, thus helping to prevent the pie crust from becoming soggy.

Method 2: instead of waxed paper and weights, the dough bottom is pricked with a fork and brushed with egg white or egg wash and baked for about 10 minutes (see Fig.2). There is a tendency for the bottom to rise slightly as the steam beneath the uncooked dough tries to escape but this can be pressed back into the pan before the filling is added. This method is better for lighter filling ingredients such as egg and herbs.

PASTRY

Some Basic Preparation Rules:
• Try not to over handle the dough. This not only makes it difficult to work with but can also encourage the gluten to over develop in the flour—ideal for bread making but not for dough. Some gluten development is important to enable the dough to have enough elasticity for rolling out —which is why a resting time is important.
• Sift the flour before adding the fat and then during the "cutting in" process, lift the mixture high above the bowl and allow to fall, to incor-

porate air, and lightness, to the finshed pie crust texture.
• When cutting-in by hand use only the finger tips as they are the coolest part of the hand.
• Any butter, shortening, milk, or water used should be chilled.
• Take care to measure the ingredients accurately—too much liquid can make the pie dough heavy or soggy, too much flour can result in a dry, tough pie crust, and too much fat makes the dough sticky and crumbly.
• Chill the pie dough for as long as possible prior to rolling out—this benefits the end texture and helps to cut down on shrinkage during baking. It also makes the dough easier to work with.

Some Basic Rolling-Out Rules
• Allow the dough to reach room temperature before rolling out as it will be easier to roll. It also means that the handling of the dough will be lessened.
• After two "rollings" gently turn the pie dough one quarter turn to assist with an even thickness and to prevent it sticking to the surface.
• Try not to dredge the surface with too much flour during rolling out as this will imbalance the ingredients and detrimentally effect the baked result. **Tip:** add the flour to either the surface of the rolling pin or beneath the rolled out dough rather than directly onto it.
• Roll out using light, even pressured strokes with the rolling pin to ensure an even thickness over the surface of the dough.
• When laying the dough into a quiche dish or tart pan, ease it in loosely from the top of the rolling pin and gently press it into the bottom and sides—particularly in a fluted edge. This prevents air spaces being left between the dough and the pan and blisters forming during baking.
• To trim any excess dough away from metal tart pans roll a rolling pin across the edge and any trimmings will simply fall away. To trim ceramic or glass dishes hold the pie on the palm of one hand and, holding a round ended knife vertically against the edge of the dish with the other hand, trim the excess.
• Keep any dough not being rolled out, covered in plastic wrap or in a small plastic bag to prevent it drying

out. This is particularly applicable when using phyllo pastry.

Some Basic Baking Rules

• Always preheat the oven prior to baking—the contrast between the difference in temperature causes the air trapped within the dough to expand faster resulting in a much lighter textured pie crust.

• Make sure that the oven temperature is correct—if it is too hot the dough will burn and if too cool it will have an undercooked, soggy texture.

• Try not to open the oven door too often during baking as this affects the temperature and therefore the end texture—particularly for puff, flaky, and cream puff doughs.

• Cover any pie edges or surfaces with aluminum foil if they start to brown too quickly—the higher oven temperature needed to ensure a crisp texture can often color the exposed dough edges too much.

DECORATIVE FINISHES

Much of the fun in making home-made pie dough is the variery of decorative finishes that can be made with pastry tools and trimmings:

Fluted pie edge: resting the tip of the thumb and forefinger of one hand on the edge of the dough, push the tip of the forefinger on the other hand against the edge to create an indent—see Fig. 3.

"V" shaped edge finishing: using the flat side of the tip of a sharp paring knife press lightly all the way round the edge of the pie crust. This not only creates a decorative rim but seals the edges together as well—see Fig. 4.

Diamond leaves: roll out some dough to a $1/4$-inch thickness. Cut into 2-inch strips. Cut across, diagonally every 2 inches to create a diamond shape. Gently score a leaf design into the top—see Fig. 4.

Tassles: take a 2-inch wide, 4-inch length of pie dough and make a series of 1-inch parallel lines across one side. Brush with egg wash before rolling the strip up and separating the pastry "fronds"—see Fig. 5.

Twists: roll two pieces of dough into long, thin sausage shapes. Lay the strips next to each other and holding one end, twist the lengths around each other. Position as required.

Lattice top: once the dough has been rolled out to desired thickness roll a lattice pastry cutter over the surface, with an even pressure and in one direction only across the dough. The resultant cuts can then be gently stretched out and egg washed before laying across the filling.

THE PASTRY RECIPES

Basic Pie Dough

A general guide when making pie dough is to use half as much fat to flour. The use of shortening will make the end texture more flaky. Instead of adding water, milk can be used to make the cooked dough softer in texture. Using self-rising flour instead of all-purpose will also have the same result.

1 cup plus 3 tablespoons all-purpose flour
6 tablespoons butter, cubed or mix of butter
  and vegetable shortening
$1/3$ cup of chilled water to mix

Fig.3

Fig.4

Fig.5

Sift the flour into a bowl. Add the butter or butter and shortening mix. Using finger tips or a pastry blender rub the fat in until the mixture resembles coarse breadcrumbs. Gradually stir in the water until the mixture binds itself together. Gently press into a ball, cover in plastic wrap, and chill for at least 20 minutes before rolling out.

NB. There will be salt contained in the butter.

Wholewheat Pie Dough

1 cup all-purpose flour
3 tablespoons wholewheat flour
6 tablespoons butter, cubed
1 egg yolk
1/4 cup chilled water to mix

Follow method as for Basic Pie Dough except once the flours have been sifted into the bowl remember to tip the grains from the wholewheat flour

Fig.6

Fig.7

Fig.8

back into the bowl. The egg yolk is mixed in prior to adding the water.

Enriched Pie Dough

1 cups plus 3 tablespoons all-purpose flour
6 tablespoons butter, cubed
2 egg large yolks
1/4 cup chilled water to mix

Method exactly as for Basic Pie Dough except where 2 egg yolks have been added the amount of water needed will reduce by approximately 2 tablespoons.

Flaky Pie Dough (Homemade version of ready-made puff pastry)

The aim here is to incorporate thin layers of fat between thin layers of dough to trap as much air as possible. In a hot oven this air expands to lift and separate each layer of dough.

1 1/2 cups all-purpose flour
3/4 cups butter or butter and shortening mix
   (6 tablespoons of each)
1/4 cup chilled water

Sift the flour into a bowl. If using butter and shortening, blend them together (when soft) and then chill for 1 hour or until firm. Divide the fat into quarters. Cut one quarter into the flour (Fig.6) and add enough cold water to form a stretchy dough. Roll the dough into a large rectangle, 15 x 8 inches, and cover two-thirds of the surface with small dabs of butter (see Fig.7).
    Fold the dough into three by bringing the fat-free end of the dough up to the center, covering some of the butter. Fold the top third of the dough over this and press edges together with finger tips (see Fig.8). Turn the dough a quarter turn and lightly roll out. Repeat the process twice more, chilling for 15 minutes between each addition of butter. Try not to over-roll as the butter will appear through the dough and become sticky. Leave to chill for 1 hour before use.

Tip: to speed up the chilling process place in the freezer for 5 minutes after each addition of butter and then for 20 minutes instead of 1 hour.

Rough Puff Dough

Based on a similar principle to Flaky

Pie Dough but uses a much quicker method.

1 1/2 cups all-purpose flour
1/2 cup plus 2 tablespoons butter or butter and shortening mix
1/4 cup of chilled water

Sift the flour. If using butter and shortening, blend while sifting and chill until firm. Cut the fat into small cubes and stir into the flour—**do not cut in**. Add enough water to bind the ingredients together to form a dough. Roll out gently to a large rectangle, 15 x 8 inches, and fold in the same way as for Flaky Pie Dough. Repeat this three or four times. Chill for 30 minutes before using.

Tip: remember to roll away from the body, not towards it, using light even strokes. Try not to break any air bubbles that may rise to the surface during the folding and resting.

Hot Water Dough

A dense, closely textured crumbly dough, which is best suited to meat-filled pies. It uses a blend of flour, shortening, and water—and a little salt. The ratio of fat to flour is much less than in other doughs resulting in its characteristic texture.

1 1/2 cups all-purpose flour
1/2 teaspoon salt
6 tablespoons shortening
1/3 cup water

Sift the flour and salt into a bowl and make a well in the center. Place the fat and water in a saucepan and heat as for Cream Puff Dough. Blend the hot mixture quickly into the flour and mix well. Knead with hands until the mixture forms a pliable dough. If the dough cools it will crack and become difficult to work with so cover any dough not being used.

Tip: it is best to have the fillings for Hot Water pies ready prior to making the dough to ensure that the dough is not left to cool for too long.

Cream Puff Dough

Most commonly used in savory Gougere recipes—a large ring of cream puff dough, which is baked, split, and filled with a cheese and vegetable sauce. This is a completely different textured dough where the air is incorporated during the addition of the beaten eggs.

4 tablespoons butter
1/2 cup water
scant 1 cup all-purpose flour, sifted
3 large eggs, beaten

Place the butter and water in a saucepan over a medium heat for 2–3 minutes until the butter has melted. Bring to a rapid boil, remove from the heat, and add all of the flour to the pan. Gradually beat in the eggs, a little at a time to obtain a smooth, glossy mixture.

Spoon or pipe the dough into balls (or the required shape) and bake in a hot oven, 400–425F (200–220C) (dependent on oven efficiency) for 10–15 minutes until risen, golden, and crisp. Pierce the bottom of the pastry with a skewer or sharp knife to allow the steam to escape and therefore prevent the dough going soggy.

OTHER PASTRIES

Ready-made puff pastry: An excellent substitute for Flaky Pie Dough when time is short.

Ready-made phyllo pastry: phyllo is extremely difficult to make by hand so it is always preferable to purchase a commercially made product. It is usually available in packs of 20 sheets, each approximately 15 x 11 inches. It is essential to keep phyllo covered with plastic wrap during preparation of the recipe or it will become dry and brittle. The fat element is incorporated by the use of melted butter being brushed over the various layers.

RECIPE NOTES

Unless otherwise mentioned:
1. Butter is salted and chilled.
2. All rolling out takes place on a lightly floured surface unless stated otherwise.
3. All quiche pans, dishes, pie plates etc should be lightly greased or buttered and floured.
4. When chilling dough it can be covered in plastic wrap or placed in a small plastic food bag.
5. Use standard measuring spoons.

QUAILS EGG TARTLETS

DOUGH:
1 recipe Basic Pie Dough (page 9)
FILLING:
16 oz mushroom medley (oyster/baby bella/button)
2 tablespoons butter
1 cup sour cream
freshly ground black pepper to taste
4 quails eggs
1 tablespoon ground almonds
few sprigs fresh tarragon

Preheat oven to 375F (190C).

Make the dough. Divide into quarters, roll out to a $1/8$-inch thickness, and use to line four $4^1/2$-inch tartlet pans. Trim any excess with a rolling pin. Roughly chop the mushrooms. Melt the butter in a large skillet and add the mushrooms. Cook for 5–7 minutes until softened. Transfer to a food processor and blend for 10 seconds. (The mushrooms should still have a rough texture.) Transfer to a bowl and stir in the sour cream. Roughly chop the tarragon, add to the mushroom mixture, and season.

Divide the mixture among the four pastry cases, making a small well in the center of the filling. Bake in the oven for 10 minutes, then remove and carefully break a quails egg into the center of each. Sprinkle a few ground almonds over the top and return to the oven for 5 minutes or until the egg is just cooked. Serve with steamed broccoli and carrots.

Makes 4

CRAB BOATS

DOUGH:
1 recipe Basic Pie Dough (page 9) replacing 4
   tablespoons of the butter with ½ cup cream cheese
   and 1 tablespoon chopped dill or tarragon, and use
   ⅓ cup milk instead of the water
FILLING:
6 sprigs fresh dill fronds
5 oz canned or fresh crabmeat
½ cup sour cream
1 large egg yolk
freshly ground black pepper to taste

Preheat the oven to 375F (190C).

Prepare the dough but after cutting in the
butter, blend the cream cheese and chopped
dill (or tarragon) into the flour with a pastry
blender. Mix in the egg yolk and enough
cold milk to bind the ingredients. Cover in
plastic wrap and chill for 15 minutes. Roll
the dough out to a ⅛-inch thickness and
cut out rough circles approximately 4 inches
in diameter. Use to line 8–10 individual
plain boat tartlet pans. Trim away excess
and prick the bottoms with a fork.

Finely chop the dill (see Filling). In a bowl,
flake the crabmeat and add the dill, sour
cream, and egg yolk. Season. Bake the boats
blind for 5 minutes then carefully spoon
small amounts of the filling into the middle.
Bake for about 10 minutes until golden
brown and the centers are slightly bubbling.

Makes 8–10

SAMBAL SAVORIES

PASTRY:
1 lb ready-made puff pastry
1/4 cup egg wash
2 teaspoons sesame seeds
2 teaspoons poppy seeds
FILLINGS:
1. 1/2 teaspoon cumin seeds
   2 small potatoes, peeled and diced
   1 small onion, finely chopped
   1/2 teaspoon turmeric powder
   1/2 teaspoon mild or hot chili powder (to taste)
2. 1/2 cup grated fresh coconut
   1 cup (5 oz) finely chopped turkey breast
   1/4 cup fresh pineapple juice
   1 teaspoon green Thai curry paste
3. 6 cherry tomatoes

1 small red bell pepper, broiled, peeled, and finely
chopped (page 81)
1 tablespoon freshly chopped cilantro

Preheat the oven to 400F (200C).

To make the fillings: 1. Add the cumin
seeds to the potatoes and mix well, then add
the chopped onion. Mix in the turmeric and
chili powder. 2. Coarsely grate the coconut
and in a separate bowl add to the turkey.
Mix in the pineapple juice and curry paste.
3. Roughly chop the tomatoes and add to
the chopped pepper. Mix in the cilantro.

SAMBAL SAVORIES

Roll the ready-made pastry out to a $1/4$-inch thickness and cut out twelve 3-inch fluted circles, six 6 x 3-inch rectangles, and six 4 x 6-inch rectangles. Lay six circles on a baking sheet and brush the edges with egg wash.

Place small mounds of the tomato filling in the center of half of the circles and top with the other circles, pressing around the edges to seal. Lay the six 3-inch rectangles on the sheet, brush the edges with egg wash, and fill one side with small mounds of the turkey filling. Fold the other half over the filling, pressing at the edges, to make a square. Fill the remaining rectangles with the potato filling along one side of the longer length and fold the other side over to make a tube. Press down at the edges to seal.

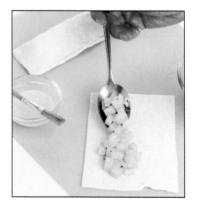

Brush the top of each savory with a little more egg wash and sprinkle with the sesame and poppy seeds. Bake for about 15 minutes until golden brown. Best served warm.

Makes 18

— ONION & PEPPER TARTLETS —

PASTRY:
8 sheets of phyllo pastry, 15 x 11-inches
FILLING:
4 tablespoons butter, melted
1 red bell pepper, seeded
1 green bell pepper, seeded
1 yellow bell pepper, seeded
2 medium red onions
1 tablespoon olive oil
2 oz feta cheese, cut into small cubes
2 large eggs
$^1/_2$ cup sour cream
freshly ground black pepper to taste

Preheat oven to 375F (190C). Grease four 4-inch plain tartlet pans with a little of the melted butter. Cut the peppers into quarters and broil under a high temperature for 3 minutes or until the skins blister and blacken. Place in a plastic bag and allow to cool. Peel away the skins and slice thinly. Cut the onions in half and slice thinly. Heat the oil in a skillet, add the onions and cook over a medium heat until soft and golden. Lay a sheet of phyllo onto a lightly floured surface and brush with melted butter.

Fold in half crosswise and lay over the top of one of the pans. Brush with butter and fold each corner into the center. Repeat for the other pans. Divide the onion and pepper mixture among the tarts and top with a few cubes of feta cheese. Blend the egg and sour cream together and season. Pour a quarter of the mixture over each tart and bake for 15 minutes until golden brown. Serve warm.

Makes 8

PIROSHKI

DOUGH:
1 recipe Enriched Pie Dough (page 10)
2 oz sun-dried tomatoes (in oil), roughly chopped
$^{1}/_{4}$ egg wash
FILLING:
6 oz cooked smoked chicken or cooked smoked
   flaked fish
1 small red onion, peeled
5 oz reduced-fat cream cheese
2 cloves garlic, peeled and crushed
1 tablespoon chopped fresh basil or parsley
freshly grated zest and juice of 1 lime
freshly ground black pepper to taste

Preheat the oven to 350F (180C). Make the dough and after cutting the butter into the flour, stir in the chopped tomatoes before adding the egg yolk and enough water to bind. Cover in plastic wrap and chill for 15 minutes. Chop the chicken or flake the fish very finely, removing any bones. Finely chop the onion and transfer to a mixing bowl. Add the cream cheese, garlic, herbs, lime juice, and zest. Stir in the chicken (or fish) and season.

Roll the dough out to a $^{1}/_{4}$-inch thickness and trim to an 8 x 10-inch rectangle. Using a metal spatula, spread the cream cheese mixture over the dough, almost to the edges, leaving a $^{1}/_{2}$-inch border. Starting at a short end, roll the dough up into a sausage shape and with a sharp knife, cut into 1-inch slices. Place on a baking sheet, brush with egg wash, and bake for 20 minutes.

Makes about 10

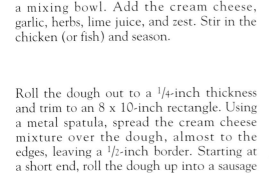

MIXED VOL-AU-VENTS

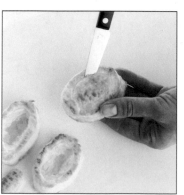

PASTRY:
10 oz ready-made puff pastry
2 tablespoons egg wash
SAUCE:
1 tablespoon each of butter and all-purpose flour
1 cup skim milk
1/3 cup grated Monterey Jack cheese (or equivalent)
freshly ground black pepper to taste
FILLINGS:
1: 2/3 cup baby asparagus tips
   2/3 cup cooked bacon, finely chopped
2: 2/3 cup tiny button mushrooms, cleaned and sliced
   2/3 cup cooked small shrimps, peeled
3: 2/3 cup hard goat cheese, diced
   1/2 roasted red bell pepper, cut into thin strips
scallions and chives to garnish

Preheat oven to 375F (190C). Roll pastry out to a 1/4-inch thickness. Cut out small ovals, 3 1/2 x 2 1/2 inches. Score a smaller oval 1/3 inch in from the edge. Place on a baking sheet. Brush with egg wash and bake for 10–15 minutes until risen and golden. Allow to cool. Steam asparagus for 2 minutes and cut into thirds. Cook the bacon in a small skillet for 2 minutes and place on a paper towel to drain. Cook the mushrooms in the same pan for 2 minutes. Heat the butter, flour, and milk over a medium heat.

Stir continuously until the sauce has thickened. Simmer for 2 minutes. Stir in the grated cheese and season. Remove the "lids" from the baked cases and spoon a teaspoon of the cheese sauce into each case. Divide each filling among four of the cases. Garnish with scallions and chives.

NOTE: If preferred, after filling, the vol-au-vents can be returned to the oven for an additional 5 minutes to warm through.

Makes 12–14

— COLCANNON SAVORY BITES —

PASTRY:
13 oz ready-made puff pastry
1 tablespoon egg wash
FILLING:
2 cups savoy cabbage
4 scallions, topped and tailed
1/2 tablespoon butter
1 teaspoon fresh ginger, peeled and finely chopped
1 teaspoon ground cumin
1 cup grated sharp cheddar cheese
1 teaspoon poppy seeds

Preheat oven to 375F (190C). Remove some of the dark outer leaves from the cabbage and shred. Steam for 2–3 minutes until softened. Cut the scallions in half and shred. Melt the butter in a small pan, taking care not to let it burn, and cook the scallions until softened. Add the scallions to the cabbage. Stir in the spices and cheese.

Roll the pastry out to a 12-inch square, 1/4-inch thick, and cut into four large triangles. Brush the edges with egg wash and divide the cabbage mixture among the rectangles placing each mound on one half of the pastry. Fold the other half over and seal with thumb and fingertips. Place on a baking sheet and brush with egg wash. Sprinkle with the poppy seeds and bake for 15–20 minutes until golden brown.

Makes 4

— PORK, SAGE, & APPLE NIBBLES —

DOUGH:
1 recipe Basic Pie Dough (page 9) but with the
    addition of 1/4 cup sour cream
1 tablespoon egg wash
FILLING:
2 medium eating apples
1 tablespoon lemon juice
8 oz pork tenderloin
1 small brown onion, finely chopped
6 large fresh sage leaves, or 1 teaspoon dried
1/2 cup apple juice
1/2 teaspoon cornstarch
freshly ground black pepper to taste

Preheat the oven to 375F (190C). Make the
dough, cover in plastic wrap, and chill for
20 minutes. Remove the cores from the
apples and quarter. Roughly chop and sprinkle with the lemon juice to prevent browning. Trim any fat from the pork and cut into
small cubes. Finely chop the sage. Blend the
apple juice and cornstarch together. Mix all
the ingredients together and season.

Roll the dough out to a 1/4-inch thickness.
Using a 4 1/2-inch diameter saucer as a guide,
cut out 10 circles. Brush the edges with egg
wash. Place a small amount of filling on one
half of the dough and fold the other half
over. Press the edges to seal. Create a flutted
(page 9). Cut out diamond shapes from the
trimmings to decorate the sides. Place on a
baking sheet, brush the tops with egg wash,
and bake for 15 minutes until golden.

Makes about 10

EGGPLANT & BEEF SHELLS

DOUGH:
1/2 cup whole almonds
3/4 cup all-purpose flour
1 large egg yolk
1/4 cup skim milk
1 tablespoon egg wash
FILLING:
4 baby eggplants
1 tablespoon lemon juice
2 tablespoons olive oil
1 medium red onion, finely chopped
8 oz fillet steak, cut into very thin strips
1 teaspoon cornstarch
1/2 cup good quality beef broth
1 small red bell pepper, broiled, peeled, and finely
   chopped (page 81)

Preheat oven to 400F (200C). To remove the almond skins place in a bowl and pour over boiling water. Soak for 5 minutes. Drain and squeeze between thumb and fore-finger to remove skins. Roast for 8 minutes in a shallow baking sheet. Cool and blend in a mini-grinder until coarsely ground. Add to flour and mix in egg yolk and milk to bind ingredients together. Cover in plastic wrap and chill for 20 minutes. Roll dough out to a 1/8-inch thickness. Line 10–12, 4-inch boat-shaped fluted tart pans. Prick with a fork, brush with egg wash.

Bake blind for 10–15 minutes until golden. Dice the eggplants and sprinkle with lemon juice to prevent browning. Heat the oil in a skillet and sauté the onion and eggplants for 5 minutes. Add the beef and fry over high heat for 2–3 minutes. Blend the cornstarch with a little broth before adding it to the remaining broth in a pan. Heat gently, stir-ring continuously until thickened. Fill the pastry shells with a little of the filling and some broth. Serve immediately.

Makes 10–12

‐ SWEET POTATO PHYLLO BITES ‐

PASTRY:
4 sheets phyllo pastry, 15 x 11-inches
2 tablespoons melted butter
FILLING:
¹/₂ small rutabaga (³/₄ cup when mashed)
2 tablespoons butter
freshly ground black pepper to taste
¹/₂ cup walnut halves
4 thin slices (1 oz) pastrami, chopped
¹/₃ cup grated sharp cheddar cheese
4 cilantro sprigs to garnish

Preheat the oven to 375F (190C). Butter a
24-cup mini-muffin pan. Peel the rutabaga
and roughly chop. Boil or steam until soft,
for about 15–20 minutes, then mash with
butter and season. Roughly chop the
walnuts and add to the rutabaga. Mix well.
Cut each sheet of phyllo into six equal
squares (keep covered under plastic wrap as
you prepare each one to prevent the pastry
drying out.)

Brush one square with a little melted butter
and press it into one of the muffin cups.
Repeat with a second square, turning it 45
degrees before placing it on top of the first
square, to make a star shape. Place a few
pieces of chopped pastrami into the bottom
of the pastry and spoon a little of the
rutabaga and nut mixture on top. Sprinkle
over some grated cheese and bake for 10
minutes until the pastry is golden and the
cheese has melted.

Makes 24

TURKEY TRIANGLES

PASTRY:
9 oz ready-made puff pastry
1 tablespoon egg wash
FILLING:
1 medium zucchini
^{1}/$_2$ tablespoon butter
1 large cooking apple, peeled, cored, and finely
  chopped
1 tablespoon granulated sugar
1^1/$_2$ cups diced turkey meat, cooked
1 cup canned corn
1–2 green jalapeño chilies, de-seeded and finely
  chopped
freshly ground black pepper to taste

Preheat oven to 375C (190C). Roll the
pastry out to a ^{1}/$_4$-inch thickness, and cut
out a 12 x 8-inch rectangle. Cut in half
lengthwise and then into three crosswise.
Cut each square in half to make two small
triangles. Brush the edges with egg wash.
Clean and trim the ends of the zucchini and
dice. Melt the butter in a small skillet and
cook the zucchini, apple, and sugar for
about 5–7 minutes until softened. Stir in the
turkey, corn, and chilies and season.

Place six of the triangles on a baking sheet
and top with small mounds of filling
mixture, leaving a ^{1}/$_4$-inch edge. Place a
remaining triangle of pastry on top of each
filling to make lids. Using the tip of a knife,
press small scores into the edge of the pastries all the way round and make a pattern
in the center with the fork prongs. Brush
tops with egg wash and bake for 15 minutes
or until until golden brown.

Makes 6

—— HAZELNUT VOL-AU-VENTS ——

PASTRY:
10 oz ready-made puff pastry
1/4 cup egg wash
FILLING:
1/3 cup dried red lentils
1 cup vegetable broth
1 tablespoon chopped fresh parsley
1/4 cup hazelnuts
2 tablespoons red currant jelly
2 or 3 parsley sprigs

Cover the lentils with water and soak for 1 hour. Drain and add them to a medium saucepan with the broth and parsley. Bring to a boil, then simmer for 25–30 minutes until soft. Drain if necessary. Preheat the oven to 400F (200C). Place the hazelnuts in a shallow roasting pan and bake for 6–7 minutes. Place them in a clean cloth and rub together to remove the skins. Roughly chop and add to the lentils. Stir in the red currant jelly and season.

Roll the pastry out to a 1/4-inch thickness to cover an 8 x 12-inch pan. Cut into 2-inch strips and then cut each strip diagonally to make small diamond shapes. Using a paring knife score a smaller diamond 1/4 inch from the edge. Place on a baking sheet and brush with egg wash. Bake for 10–12 minutes until golden and risen. Remove the centers from the pastry diamonds and fill with a little filling. Garnish with a few parsley sprigs and serve.

Makes about 18

BEAN & CORN TARTLETS

DOUGH:
1 cup all-purpose flour
¹/₂ cup fine cornmeal
¹/₂ cup butter, cubed
1 large egg yolk
¹/₂ cup water (to mix)
FILLING:
1 cup small green beans, chopped
scant 1 cup canned lima beans (drained)
¹/₂ cup canned corn
1 cup 2% milk
1 tablespoon each of butter and all-purpose flour
1 cup blue cheese, crumbled
freshly ground black pepper to taste
1 egg yolk
2 thick smoked bacon slices (topping)

Preheat oven to 375F (190C). Make the dough as described on page 77. Bring a small pan of slightly salted water to a boil and cook the green beans for 5 minutes. Drain into a colander and place under cold running water for 10 seconds. Place in a bowl with the lima beans and corn. Add the milk, butter, and flour to a small saucepan. Whisk over a medium heat until thickened. Mix in the blue cheese and season. Beat in the egg yolk.

Roll the dough out to a ¹/₄-inch thickness, and line four 4 x 1¹/₂-inch individual loose-bottomed tartlet pans. Prick the bottom of each pie crust with a fork and bake blind for 5 minutes. Add the beans to the cheese sauce and spoon into the tartlets. Bake for 15–20 minutes until golden. Heat a small skillet over a high heat and add the chopped bacon. Cook for 5 minutes until crispy. Remove the tartlets from their pans and top each with a quarter of the bacon pieces.

Makes 4

BACON & EGG PASTIES

DOUGH:
6 tablespoons butter, cubed
1 cup plus 2 tablespoons all-purpose flour
8 basil leaves, roughly chopped
2 tablespoons canned tomato paste and herb sauce
1 tablespoon egg wash
FILLING:
1 teaspoon corn oil or canola oil
1 medium brown onion, roughly chopped
6 oz Canadian bacon slices, roughly chopped
1 large egg, beaten
freshly ground black pepper to taste

Preheat oven to 375F (190C). Using a pastry blender, mix the butter into the flour until it resembles breadcrumbs. Stir in the basil and tomato paste and mix to a dough. Cover in plastic wrap and chill for 15 minutes. Heat the oil in a skillet and sauté the onion for approximately 2 minutes until softened. Add the bacon and cook for an additional 2 minutes. Stir in the beaten egg and season.

Roll the dough out to a $^{1}/_{4}$-inch thickness and cut out 6 rectangles, 6 x $4^{1}/_{2}$ inches. Brush the egg wash around the edges of the dough and divide the filling among the rectangles, placing it on one half of the dough. Fold the other half over the filling and seal the edges with the back of a fork. Place on a baking sheet and brush the top with egg wash before baking for 15 minutes, until crisp to the touch.

Makes 6

—— LAMB & TOMATO TWISTS ——

PASTRY:
10 oz ready-made puff-pastry
1 tablespoon egg wash
FILLING:
1¼ cups (6 oz) cooked lamb pieces
10 cherry tomatoes, washed and halved
10 mint leaves
freshly ground black pepper to taste

Preheat oven to 375F (190C). Blend the lamb, tomatoes, and mint together in a food processor to form a thick paste and season.

On a lightly floured surface roll the pastry out to make a 12-inch square, ¼-inch thick. Lightly brush the surface with egg wash and then cut into eight 1½-inch strips.

Spread a little of the paste along each strip and then holding one end of the pastry twist the strip. Place on a baking sheet and bake for 10–15 minutes until golden brown.

Makes 8

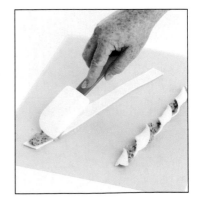

MINI PORK TURNOVERS

DOUGH:
1 recipe Hot Water Dough (page 11)
$^1/_4$ cup egg wash
FILLING:
6 oz lean pork tenderloin
1 medium parsnip, peeled and diced
1 small brown onion, diced
$^1/_2$ teaspoon ground cloves, plus extra for sprinkling
$^1/_2$ teaspoon paprika
$^1/_2$ teaspoon dried chili flakes
freshly ground black pepper to taste

Preheat oven to 400F (200C). Divide the dough into six equal portions. While making each turnover, keep the remaining dough covered (with plastic wrap or in a small plastic bag) to prevent it drying out. Cut the pork tenderloin into $^1/_2$-inch cubes. Mix all filling ingredients together and season.

Roll each portion of dough out to $^1/_4$-inch thickness, and make a 6 x 3-inch rectangle. Brush the edges with egg wash and place $^1/_6$ of the filling mixture on one side of each piece of dough. Fold the other half over to make a square, pressing down on the edges to seal. Place on a baking sheet and brush with egg wash. Sprinkle with a little ground cloves and bake for 15–20 minutes until crisp and golden brown.

Makes 6

LUXURY FISH PIE

PASTRY:
8 oz ready-made puff pastry
TOPPING:
1 cup new potatoes
1 cup parsnips
1 cup grated sharp cheddar cheese
FILLING:
1 lb mixture of fish, shrimp, and sea scallops
1 small lemon
1 small parsnip, peeled and cubed
2 shallots, peeled and chopped
6 black peppercorns
2 bay leaves
2¼ cups 2% milk
4 tablespoons butter
6 tablespoons all-purpose flour

²/₃ cup mild cheddar cheese, grated
2 tablespoons freshly chopped dill
freshly ground black pepper to taste

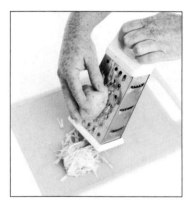

Preheat oven to 375F (190C). Grate the potatoes and parsnips for the topping. Cut the fish into 1-inch chunks, removing any bones. Devein the shrimp. Squeeze lemon over fish and season. Place the parsnip, shallots, peppercorns, and bay leaves for the filling into a saucepan with the milk. Bring to a gentle simmer for 5 minutes.

Strain the milk, discarding the vegetables. Melt the butter in a pan and add the flour. Cook for 2 minutes before gradually adding the milk, stirring constantly. Mix in the cheese and chopped dill. Add the fish, shrimp, and scallops and season. Roll the pastry out to ¼-inch thickness and use to line the dish. Trim the edges. Spoon the fish mixture into the pastry shell. Scatter the grated potatoes, parsnip, and cheese over the fish and bake for 35–40 minutes.

Serves 4

RABBIT PIE

DOUGH:
1 recipe Enriched Pie Dough (page 10) with 1
 tablespoon chopped fresh parsley and 5 sage leaves,
 chopped
1 tablespoon egg wash
FILLING:
3 lb rabbit, portioned
1 tablespoon canola oil
16 small shallots
1 tablespoon brown sugar
$^1/_2$ cup red wine
1 cup chicken broth
1 bay leaf
1 large sprig fresh rosemary
$^1/_4$ cup juniper berries

Preheat oven to 375F (190C). Make the
dough, adding in the chopped herbs after
cutting the butter into the flour. Cover in
plastic wrap and chill until needed. Heat
the oil in a Dutch oven and add the (whole)
shallots. Cook for 2–3 minutes before
adding the brown sugar and continue
cooking until browned/glazed, for about 5
minutes. Add the rabbit and brown. Add all
the remaining ingredients (using $^3/_4$ of the
broth) and cover. Bring to a gentle simmer,
transfer to the oven, and cook for about $1^1/_2$
hours, stirring once or twice.

If the casserole starts to dry add a little more
of the reserved stock. Transfer the rabbit
and sauce to a 2-inch deep, 9-inch oval pie
dish. Roll the dough out to a $^1/_4$-inch thickness, using the pie dish as a size guide, but
rolling 1 inch larger. Make a pastry collar to
sit on edge of dish, then cover with the
remaining oval of pastry, pressing down
around the edge to seal. Make a small cut in
the center, brush with egg wash, and bake
for 25–30 minutes until pastry is golden.

Serves 4

FAMILY CHICKEN PIE

DOUGH:
1 recipe Flaky Pie Dough (page 10)
1/4 cup egg wash
FILLING:
4 (6-oz) skinless, boneless chicken breasts
1/2 lemon
1 large onion
2 medium carrots
5 oz broccoli
3 oz sweet corn kernels
SAUCE:
1 small onion, sliced
1 small carrot, peeled and roughly chopped
1 stick celery, washed and sliced
4 peppercorns

2 1/2 cups 2% milk
2 tablespoons butter
3 tablespoons all-purpose flour
freshly ground black pepper to taste

Preheat oven to 375F (190C). Place the chicken in a roasting pan, squeeze over the lemon juice. Cook for 25 minutes, until the juices run clear. Cut into large chunks. Chop the onion, peel and slice the carrots, and cut the broccoli into florets. Blanch for 5 minutes: set aside. In a pan, add the vegetables and peppercorns to the milk for sauce.

Bring to a boil and simmer for 5 minutes. Drain, reserving the milk. Clean the pan, return the milk, and add the butter and flour. Whisk over a medium heat until thickened. Add the chicken and blanched vegetables, season. Transfer to a 9-inch pie dish and butter the edges. Roll out the dough on a heavily floured surface (1/4-inch thick) and cover the filling. Trim excess, brush the edges with egg wash, and bake for 40–45 minutes.

Serves 4

BEEF & MUSHROOM PIE

DOUGH:
1 recipe Basic Pie Dough (page 9)
1 tablespoon egg wash
FILLING:
1 lb beef chuck steak
1 tablespoon olive oil
2 medium red onions, chopped
$^{1}/_{2}$ cup red wine
1 cup meat broth
4 oz baby bella mushrooms, cleaned and quartered
1 tablespoon chopped mixed fresh herbs

Preheat oven to 325F (160C).

Cut the steak into 1-inch cubes, discarding any fat. Heat the oil in an ovenproof pan and sauté the onions for 2 minutes before adding the meat. Cook until browned, then add the red wine and broth. Cover and cook in the oven for 1 hour or until tender. Remove from the oven and stir in the mushrooms and herbs. Allow to cool. Divide the dough into thirds. Roll out two-thirds of the dough ($^{1}/_{8}$-inch thick). Use to line a 9-inch pie pan and trim the edges. Brush the top edges of the dough with egg wash and spoon in the beef mixture.

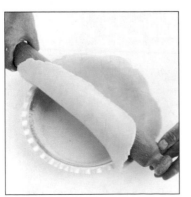

Roll out the third piece of dough to make a lid and use to cover the filling. Using a crimping wheel, make a decorative pattern on the top of the pie. Brush with egg wash and bake for 35–40 minutes until golden brown.

NOTES: cover the edges with aluminum foil if they start to brown too quickly.

Serves 4

— QUICK VEAL, HAM, & EGG PIE —

DOUGH:
1 recipe Hot Water Dough (page 11)
1 tablespoon egg wash
FILLING:
5 oz veal scallop
4 oz thick ham steak
1 tablespoon sunflower oil
1 small brown onion, finely chopped
2 large hard-boiled eggs
2 tablespoons fine-cut relish, e.g. cocktail gherkins, finely chopped
1 tablespoon chopped fresh herbs, e.g. parsley or thyme
freshly ground black pepper to taste

Preheat oven to 400F (200C). Make the dough and divide into thirds. Keep one-third wrapped in plastic wrap and roll the remaining dough out to a circle slightly larger than needed to line a deep 2 1/4-cup baking dish. Cut the veal and ham into 1/2-inch cubes. Heat the oil in a small skillet and cook the onion and meat for 10 minutes, over a medium heat, until browned. Roughly chop and add the hard-boiled eggs to the onion and meat. Mix in the gherkins and herbs and season.

Generously butter the dish and line with the rolled-out dough, leaving a 1/2-inch overhang. Spoon in the filling and level with the back of a spoon. Roll the third piece of dough out to a 1/4-inch thickness to make a lid. Press the edges down to seal and cut a small hole in the center to allow steam to escape. Use any trimmings for decoration. Brush the top with egg wash and bake for 35–40 minutes, covering with aluminum foil if the pastry starts to brown too quickly.

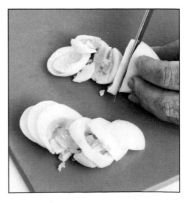

Serves 4

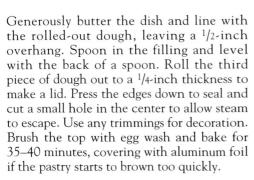

— CHICKEN & MUSHROOM PIE —

DOUGH:
1 1/2 recipes Enriched Pie Dough (page 10)
1 tablespoon egg wash
FILLING:
1 lb skinless, boneless, chicken breast
1 tablespoon each of canola oil and unsalted butter
6 oz brown mushrooms, cleaned and quartered
2 cups 2% milk
1 small carrot, peeled and roughly chopped
1 celery stick, washed
1 small onion, sliced
1 bay leaf
4 black peppercorns
1 tablespoon cornstarch mixed with 2 tablespoons water
1 tablespoon chopped fresh Italian parsley

Make the dough, cover in plastic wrap, and chill for 20 minutes. Preheat oven to 375F (190C). Cut the chicken into 1/2-inch cubes. Heat the oil in a skillet and cook the chicken for 5–8 minutes until white then transfer to a plate. Sauté the mushrooms with the butter for 5 minutes. Put the milk, carrot, celery, onion, bay leaf, and peppercorns in a saucepan. Bring to a boil and simmer gently for 5 minutes. Strain milk into a clean saucepan.

Stir the cornstarch mixture into the milk. Cook, stirring until thickened then add the parsley, chicken, and mushrooms. Allow to cool. Roll out two-thirds of the dough to a 1/4-inch thickness and line the bottom of a 9-inch pie plate. Trim the excess, brush the edges with egg wash, and add the filling. Roll out the remaining dough to make a lid. Press edges with a knife tip to seal. Brush the edges with egg wash and bake for 40–45 minutes.

Serves 4

— LAMB, POTATO, & BEAN PIE —

DOUGH:
1 recipe Flaky Pie Dough (page 10) but use 1 cup
  all-purpose flour and 6 tablespoons butter
1 tablespoon egg wash
FILLING:
1 lb 2 oz tomatoes, roughly chopped
1 tablespoon granulated sugar
$^1/_2$ teaspoon sea salt
freshly ground black pepper to taste
1 tablespoon chopped fresh parsley
1$^1/_4$ lb boneless lamb
1 medium onion, roughly chopped
1 tablespoon olive oil
1 tablespoon cayenne pepper or paprika
2–3 fresh rosemary sprigs
1 (16 oz) can cannellini beans, drained
8 oz baby new potatoes, washed and halved

Make the dough, cover in plastic wrap, and chill for 1 hour. Preheat oven to 400F (200C). Place the tomatoes in a pan with the sugar, salt, and season. Cook for 20 minutes on a low heat, until soft, stirring occasionally. Pass through a wire mesh sieve or alternatively blend in a food processor and then pass through a sieve to remove skin and seeds. Stir in the chopped parsley and season. Trim any excess fat from the lamb and cut into $^1/_2$-inch cubes. Heat the oil and add the lamb and onion.

Cook for 10 minutes until browned. Add tomato sauce, cayenne (or paprika), rosemary, beans, and potatoes. Cover and simmer for 20 minutes on a low heat, stirring occasionally. Transfer to a buttered 9-inch pie plate. Roll the dough out on a heavily floured surface ($^1/_4$ inch thick), to the size of the pie dish, and cover. Make a small cut in the surface, brush with egg wash, and bake for 35–40 minutes until golden brown.

Serves 4–6

SURPRISE PARCEL PIE

DOUGH:
1 recipe Rough Puff Dough (page 10)
FILLING:
²/₃ cup brown rice
1 teaspoon Worcestershire sauce
6 oz ground pork
2 large shallots, roughly chopped
1 tablespoon chopped fresh sage
¹/₃ cup golden raisins
8 savoy cabbage leaves
2 large eggs
¹/₃ cup 2% milk
freshly ground black pepper to taste
1 oz wholewheat breadcrumbs
¹/₃ cup grated sharp cheddar cheese
5 cherry tomatoes, halved

Preheat oven to 375F (190C). Make the pastry using a pastry blender to cut ¹/₃ of the fat into the flour, then proceed as on page 10. Place the rice in a pan with 1 cup of water and the Worcestershire sauce. Bring to a boil and simmer for 20 minutes. Strain. In a nonstick skillet cook the ground pork for 5 minutes. Add the shallots and sage and cook for 5 minutes. Stir in the golden raisins. Remove the tough stalks from the cabbage and place in a pan of boiling, slightly salted water. Cook for 5–10 minutes, until softened. Drain and cool.

Roll the dough out (¹/₄ inch thick) and line an 8-inch loose-bottomed quiche pan and trim excess. Take a single cabbage leaf and place a mound of filling in the center. Fold the edges over the filling and place in the dish. Repeat with the other leaves to fill the bottom. Blend the eggs and milk together and season. Pour over the cabbage parcels. Arrange the tomatoes on top, cover with the breadcrumbs and cheese. Bake for 30–35 minutes until the crust is golden brown.

Serves 4

PHYLLO CROUSTADE

PASTRY:
6 sheets phyllo pastry, 15 x 11-inches
2 tablespoons melted butter
FILLING:
16 oz peeled and diced rutabaga
1 tablespoon butter
freshly ground black pepper to taste
8 oz smoked haddock fillet
1 cup skim milk
1 bay leaf
SAUCE:
1 cup skim milk
4 tablespoons butter
4 tablespoons all-purpose flour
⅔ cup grated sharp cheddar cheese
freshly ground black pepper to taste

Preheat oven to 350F (180C). Boil or steam the rutabaga until soft and then mash with the butter. Season. Cut the haddock in half and place in an ovenproof dish. Pour the milk over the fish, add the bay leaf, cover, and cook in oven for 20 minutes until fish is opaque and flakes easily. Transfer to a bowl, remove the skin, and flake. Strain the cooking milk into a clean saucepan. Add the rest of the milk (see Sauce), butter, and flour, and whisk over a medium heat until thickened. Simmer for 2 minutes and stir in the cheese, seasoning to taste.

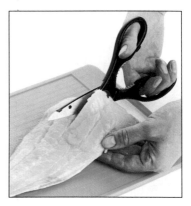

Brush each sheet of phyllo with melted butter, fold in half across the width and build up overlapping layers in the bottom of a lightly buttered 8-inch pie dish (about 3 sheets on each side). Spoon the mashed rutabaga on top of the pastry and then add the haddock. Pour over the cheese sauce and bake for 20–25 minutes until golden.

Serves 4

LAMB PHYLLO FANCY

PASTRY:
6–7 sheets phyllo pastry, 15 x 11-inches
2 tablespoons melted butter
FILLING:
1 lb lean lamb
1 tablespoon canola oil
1 medium brown onion, finely chopped
2 garlic cloves, crushed
zest and juice of 1 large orange
14 oz canned, diced plum tomatoes
2 green chilies, seeded, and finely chopped
1 teaspoon jerk seasoning (or ground allspice)
1 tablespoon chopped fresh cilantro and parsley
$^{1}/_{2}$ cup sour cream
freshly ground black pepper to taste

Preheat oven to 375F (190C). Trim away any fat from the meat and cut into cubes. Heat the oil in a skillet and add the onion. Cook for 2–3 minutes and add the garlic and lamb. Cook for an additional 5 minutes and then add the orange zest and juice, tomatoes, chilies, and jerk seasoning. Cook on a very low heat for about 45 minutes until tender, stirring occasionally. Stir in the herbs and sour cream. Taste and add more seasoning or black pepper if desired. Spoon into a 9-inch pie dish.

Take a sheet of phyllo and brush with melted butter, fold in half, cut into two squares, brush with more butter, and fold into a triangle. "Concertina" the pastry to create a decorative effect and lay on top of the filling. Repeat with as many pieces as needed to cover the top. Bake in the oven for approximately 20 minutes or until top is crispy and golden brown.

Serves 4

– VEGETARIAN CORNBREAD PIE –

DOUGH:
3/4 cup all-purpose flour
1/3 cup fine cornmeal (or masa harina)
6 tablespoons butter, cubed
1 tablespoon chopped fresh cilantro
1 large egg yolk plus 1 tablespoon egg wash
1/3 cup buttermilk or sour cream
FILLING:
1 1/4 cups tofu or soy bean curd
grated zest and juice of 1 orange
1-inch piece of fresh ginger, peeled
1 medium leek, trimmed
1 tablespoon each of butter and cornstarch
1 large red onion, roughly chopped
2 garlic cloves, peeled and crushed
1 1/2 cups or 1 (14-oz) can cannellini beans, drained

1/2 cup plus 1 tablespoon orange juice
freshly ground black pepper to taste

Preheat oven to 375F (190C). Cube the tofu and place in a bowl. Add zest and orange juice. Cut the ginger into thin strips and add. Marinate for 1 hour. Place the flour, cornmeal, and butter in a bowl and cut in until it resembles coarse breadcrumbs. Add the cilantro, egg yolk, buttermilk, and 1/4 cup water to bind. Cover with plastic wrap and chill for 20 minutes. Thickly slice the leek. Melt the butter in a skillet.

Sauté the leek, onion, and garlic for 5 minutes until softened. Mix in the beans. Remove the tofu from the marinade and add. Blend the cornstarch with a tablespoon of orange juice until smooth then add the remaining marinade. Pour over filling and stir over a medium heat until thickened. Transfer to a 9-inch oval (2-inch deep) pie dish. Roll the dough out to 1/4-inch thickness and place over filling. Trim excess, brush with egg wash, and bake for 30 minutes until golden.

Serves 4–6

FRITTATA PIE

PASTRY:
12 oz ready-made puff pastry
1 tablespoon egg wash
FILLING:
1 medium zucchini, cleaned and trimmed
3 cups broccoli florets
1 tablespoon canola oil
1 medium red onion, sliced
3 large eggs
1 cup ricotta cheese
1/4 cup 2% milk
1 tablespoon chopped fresh basil
1/2 cup chopped pastrami
1/4 cup chopped salami
freshly ground black pepper to taste

2 medium tomatoes, sliced and halved
1/4 cup grated Emmental or Gruyere cheese
1 tablespoon sesame seeds

Preheat oven to (400F) (200C). Roll out two-thirds of the pastry (1/4 inch thick) and line a 9-inch (2-inch deep) pie dish. Brush edges with egg wash. Cut the zucchini into cubes. Steam the zucchini and broccoli for 5–6 minutes. Heat the oil in a small skillet and sauté the onion for 8 minutes until just browned. Spoon into the pastry case. Top with the zucchini and broccoli.

Blend the eggs, ricotta, and milk together. Stir in the basil, pastrami, and salami. Season. Pour into the pastry shell. Place the tomatoes on top and sprinkle the cheese over. Roll the remaining pastry out, using the pie dish as a size guide. Press across the surface with a lattice pastry cutter and stretch across the filling. Trim the edges. Brush surface with egg wash and sprinkle with sesame seeds. Bake for 35–40 minutes until golden brown and the filling has set.

Serves 4–6

BUTTERNUT SQUASH PIE

DOUGH:
1 recipe Flaky Pie Dough (page 10)
1 tablespoon egg wash
FILLING:
1 garlic clove, peeled and crushed
1/2 butternut squash, seeded
1 tablespoon olive oil
1/2 teaspoon sea salt flakes
1 small brown onion, chopped
2/3 cups Arborio (risotto) rice
1/2 cup white wine
1/2 cup vegetable broth
freshly ground black pepper to taste
TOPPING:
1 oz (1 slice) white bread
2 graham crackers

1 tablespoon chopped fresh parsley
1/3 cup grated Monterey Jack cheese

Preheat oven to 400F (200C). Spread the garlic over the cut surface of the squash and drizzle with half of the oil. Sprinkle with the salt and open roast for 40–45 minutes until soft inside. Remove from the skin and mash. Heat the remaining oil and sauté the onion for 2 minutes. Add the rice and cook for 1 minute. Gradually add in the wine and broth, stirring continually, until all the liquid has been absorbed and the rice is tender. (Add more water if necessary).

Stir the mashed squash into the rice and season to taste. Roll the dough out (1/4 inch thick) and line an 8-inch pie dish with the dough. Bake blind for 10 minutes then spoon the rice mixture into the bottom of the pie crust. Place the bread, crackers, parsley, and cheese into a food processor and blend until the mixture has turned to crumbs. Sprinkle over the top of the pie and bake for 30–35 minutes until crust is golden.

Serves 4

— CHRISTMAS CROISSANT RING —

DOUGH:
2 cans ready-made croissant dough
¼ cup egg wash
1 tablespoon sesame seeds
FILLING:
2 cups (10 oz) cubed, cooked turkey or chicken
4 scallions, trimmed
¼ cup mayonnaise
¼ cup sour cream
1 tablespoon chopped fresh parsley
¼ cup cranberry sauce
freshly ground black pepper to taste

Preheat the oven to 350F (180C). Place the meat in a large mixing bowl. Open the cans of croissant dough and separate them into triangles. Arrange the triangles on a baking sheet, slightly overlapping, to create a ring or star of about a 14-inch diameter.

Slice the scallions thinly.

— CHRISTMAS CROISSANT RING —

Add the scallions to the turkey (or chicken), along with the mayonnaise, sour cream, parsley, and cranberry sauce. Mix well and season.

Brush the croissant "star" with egg wash and spoon the filling onto the widest part of the triangles. Fold the tips over to cover the filling and tuck in slightly.

Brush the top with egg wash and sprinkle with sesame seeds. Bake for 25–30 minutes until golden brown. If desired, serve with a green salad and radishes.

Serves 10

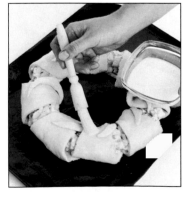

SPICY SAUSAGE PIE

DOUGH:
1 cup less 2 tablespoons all-purpose flour
2 tablespoons butter, cubed
1 tablespoon chopped fresh thyme
²/₃ cup grated sharp cheddar cheese
1 large egg yolk
¹/₃ cup cold water to mix
1 tablespoon egg wash
FILLING:
4 Italian sausages with herbs
6 large shallots, peeled and halved
1 cup canned tomato sauce with herbs
2 oz thin slices pepperoni

Preheat the oven to 375F (190C).

Place the flour, butter, thyme, and cheese into a food processor and pulse until blended. Add the egg yolk and enough water to bind (using the pulse action). Wrap in plastic wrap and chill for 15 minutes. Cook the sausages in a skillet over a medium heat until browned (about 6–8 minutes). Remove to a plate and cook the shallots for 5 minutes. Thickly slice the sausages and add to a mixing bowl with the shallots. Stir in the tomato sauce and pepperoni and transfer to a shallow 8-inch pie dish. Butter the edges.

Roll the dough out to fit the pie dish. Cover the filling and trim away any excess dough. Use the trimmings to make some leaves and a tassle (page 9). Brush the dough with egg wash and bake in the oven for about 25 minutes until crisp and golden.

Serves 4

NOTE: to double the recipe to serve 2 sausages per person, simply use a deep pie dish instead of shallow.

LOUISIANA MOUSSAKA

DOUGH:
1 recipe Enriched Pie Dough (page 10) minus 1 egg
  yolk but adding 1 teaspoon Tabasco sauce and
  ¹/4 cup sour cream
1 tablespoon egg wash
FILLING:
1 lb each of tomatoes and lean chuck steak
1 tablespoon each of canola oil and olive oil
1 large red onion, roughly chopped
1¹/4 cups beef broth
1 tablespoon hot chili powder
2 green jalapeño chilies, seeded and finely chopped
1 (10-oz) can pinto beans, drained
1 (10-oz) can kidney beans, drained
¹/2 small lemon
1 small eggplant, thinly sliced

Preheat oven to 375F (190C). Make the
dough but after cutting in the butter, stir in
the Tabasco and sour cream. Add enough
cold water to bind, cover with plastic wrap,
and chill for 15 minutes. Cut a small cross
in the top of the tomatoes and place in a
bowl. Cover with boiling water and leave
for 5 minutes. Drain, cool, and remove
skins. Pass through a mesh sieve. Heat the
oil in a large saucepan and add the onion.
Cook for 2 minutes until soft then add the
steak. Cook for 5–6 minutes until browned.

Add the tomatoes, broth, chili powder, and
chilies. Simmer gently for 40 minutes,
stirring occasionally. Add the beans and
mix well. Transfer to an 11-inch oval pie
dish (2 inches deep). Squeeze the lemon
over the eggplant. Heat the olive oil in a
skillet and brown eggplant on both sides.
Arrange over the filling. Roll the dough out
(¹/4 inch thick) and cover the filling. Brush
with egg wash and then bake for 25–30
minutes until golden.

Serves 4

— LARDON, LEEK, & POTATO PIE —

DOUGH:
1 recipe Flaky Pie Dough (page 10)
FILLING:
1 medium leek
2 medium potatoes
7-oz piece lean bacon
2 tablespoons drawn butter
1/2 cup skim milk
1/3 cup light cream
2 large eggs, beaten
2 teaspooons dried mixed herbs
2/3 cup grated cheddar cheese
freshly ground black pepper to taste

Preheat the oven to 375F (190C). Cut the leek in half lengthwise and slice thickly. Place in a colander and wash thoroughly under running water to clean. Peel and thinly slice the potatoes. Place in a bowl of water. Roll the dough out to 1/4-inch thickness and line an 8-inch diameter, 2-inch deep, springform pan. Trim the excess dough.

Trim away any bacon rind and roughly chop the bacon. Cook in a small skillet for 5 minutes and transfer to a dish lined with paper towel. Cook the leeks in the same pan until just softened. In a larger skillet, heat the butter and cook the potato slices in two batches until lightly browned.

— LARDON, LEEK, & POTATO PIE —

Spoon the bacon into the pie crust and cover with the leeks.

Starting from the outside, arrange the potato slices in an overlapping circle to cover the leeks completely.

Beat together the milk, cream, eggs, and herbs, and season. Slowly pour over the pie layers and top with grated cheese. Bake for 40–45 minutes, covering with aluminum foil if the top starts to brown too quickly.

Serves 4

SUPPER TIME QUICHE

DOUGH:
1 recipe Enriched Pie Dough (page 10)
FILLING:
2 cups broccoli florets
1 cup (5 oz) cubed ham
SAUCE:
¼ cup skim milk
1½ tablespoons all-purpose flour
1 tablespoon butter
⅔ cup grated sharp cheddar cheese
freshly ground black pepper to taste
TOPPING:
2 tablespoons wholewheat breadcrumbs
⅓ cup grated sharp cheddar cheese

Preheat the oven to 350F (180C). Lightly butter and flour a 10-inch loose-based quiche pan. Make the dough. Cover in plastic wrap and chill for 20 minutes. Drop broccoli into a pan of boiling water and simmer for 5–8 minutes then plunge into a bowl of cold water for 1 minute and drain. To make the cheese sauce whisk the milk, flour, and butter in a saucepan over a medium heat until thickened. Simmer for 2 minutes and then stir in the cheese. Season.

Roll the dough out to ¼-inch thickness and line the pan. Trim, leaving a small over-hang. Bake blind for 10 minutes. Remove the waxed paper and weights and return the pie crust to the oven for another 10 minutes until cooked and golden. Place the broccoli and ham into the pie shell and pour the cheese sauce over the top. Cover with the breadcrumbs and broil for 10 minutes under a medium broiler.

Serves 4

RED ONION QUICHE

DOUGH:
1 recipe Flaky Pie Dough (page 10)
FILLING:
1 tablespoon canola oil
1 large red onion, halved and sliced
1 medium brown onion, halved and sliced
2 garlic cloves, peeled and crushed
8 oz small waxy potatoes, peeled
4 large eggs
1¼ cups skim milk
1 tablespoon chopped fresh Italian parsley
freshly ground black pepper to taste

Preheat the oven to 400F (200C). Heat the oil in a large skillet and sauté the onions for 5 minutes. Add the garlic and cook for an additional minute. Slice the potatoes thinly and soak in a bowl of cold water for 10 minutes to remove some of the starch, and to prevent the potatoes from sticking together too much during cooking.

On a heavily floured surface roll the dough out to ¼-inch thickness to fit a 9-inch quiche dish, leaving a little overhanging the rim. Arrange the onion in the bottom of the quiche and lay the drained potato slices on top. Beat the eggs, milk, parsley, and seasoning together and pour over the onion and potatoes. Trim the pastry around the edges slightly. Bake for 40–45 minutes until golden and the filling is set.

Serves 4–6

— THREE-WAY TOMATO QUICHE —

DOUGH:
1 cup all-purpose flour
1/2 teaspoon turmeric
generous 1/3 cup butter
1 tablespoon tomato paste
FILLING:
1/2 small rutabagas, peeled and cubed
2 tablespoons butter
6 basil leaves, roughly torn
freshly ground black pepper to taste
1 large egg, plus 2 yolks
1/4 cup tomato sauce with garlic and herbs
scant 2 cups mixed beans, drained
3 medium tomatoes, washed and sliced
1/3 cup grated sharp cheddar
1/2 cup arugula leaves to garnish

Preheat the oven to 375F (190C). Sift flour into a bowl and mix in turmeric. Cut the butter into the flour until mixture resembles coarse breadcrumbs. Blend tomato sauce with 1/4 cup cold water and stir into the flour until it forms a dough. Cover in plastic wrap and chill for 15 minutes. Boil or steam the rutabaga and mash with the butter. Stir in the basil and season. Add egg and yolks to the tomato paste and stir in the beans.

Roll the dough out 1/4 inch thick and use to line a 9-inch quiche pan. Trim the edges. Brush bottom with about 1 teaspoon of egg white, prick with a fork, and bake for 10 minutes. Spoon the rutabaga into the bottom and the bean mixture over the top. Arrange the tomato slices on the top and sprinkle with the grated cheese. Bake for 40–45 minutes, covering with aluminum foil for the last 20 minutes to prevent the top burning. Garnish with arugula leaves.

Serves 4

FINNISH MEAT QUICHE

DOUGH:
1 recipe Flaky Pie Dough (page 10)
FILLING:
5 oz ground beef
5 oz ground pork
1 medium brown onion, halved and sliced
3/4 cup meat broth
1/3 cup heavy cream
1 tablespoon paprika
1 tablespoon chopped fresh Italian parsley
1/3 cup brown rice
1 large egg, beaten
2/3 cup grated sharp cheddar cheese
freshly ground black pepper to taste

Make the dough. Cover in plastic wrap and chill for 1 hour. Preheat oven to 400F (200C). Heat a large nonstick skillet and cook the beef and pork until browned, 6–8 minutes. Transfer to a plate lined with paper towel and wipe the pan clean of excess fat. Add the onion and sauté for 5 minutes, then stir in 1/3 cup of the broth and return the mince to the pan. Add the cream, paprika, and parsley. Rinse the rice and add to another saucepan with the remaining broth. Bring to a boil and then simmer for 15 minutes, until the rice is al dente.

Drain and place a piece of paper towel over the pan briefly to absorb excess moisture. Stir the rice into the meat mixture along with the beaten egg. Season. Roll the dough to 1/4-inch thickness, use to line a 9-inch quiche pan. Bake blind for 10 minutes. Spoon the filling into the pastry and top with grated cheese. Reduce the oven temperature to 375F (190C). Bake for 40–45 minutes, covering the top with foil if it starts to brown too quickly.

Serves 4

— SPINACH & RICOTTA QUICHE —

DOUGH:
1 1/2 cups all-purpose flour
3 tablespoons wholewheat flour
1/2 cup vegetable shortening, cubed
1/2 cup butter, cubed
1 egg yolk and 1/4 cup chilled water to bind
FILLING:
1/4 cup pine kernels
1 tablespoon sunflower oil
1 red onion, halved and sliced
10 oz spinach leaves, washed
1 cup ricotta cheese
1/3 cup skim milk
1 large egg, beaten
1 teaspoon freshly grated nutmeg
1/3 cup grated Emmental or equivalent Swiss cheese

Preheat oven to 375F (190C). Blend vegetable shortening and butter into the flours. Add the yolk and cold water to form a soft dough. Cover in plastic wrap and chill for 20 minutes. In a small skillet over a medium heat, roast the pine kernels until just brown. Transfer to a plate. Sauté the onion in the same skillet in a little oil. In a larger skillet cook the spinach until just wilted and stir in the ricotta cheese. Reserving 1 teaspoon of the beaten egg, add remainder to the pan, along with the milk, nutmeg, and pepper.

Roll the dough into a long rectangular shape, 1/4 inch thick, slightly larger than the pan. Using the rolling pin, lay the dough into a 15 x 5-inch pan. Press into the bottom and trim excess. Brush the bottom of the tart with the reserved egg and bake for 5 minutes. Arrange the onion in the bottom and spoon the spinach mixture over the top. Sprinkle the pine kernels and cheese over the surface and bake for 30–35 minutes until golden brown and set.

Serves 6

ASPARAGUS & WALNUT QUICHE

DOUGH:
1 recipe Basic Pie Dough (page 9)
1 tablespoon tomato paste
FILLING:
1 tablespoon canola oil
1 medium leek, washed and sliced
2 cloves garlic, peeled
1½ cups asparagus tips, halved
¼ cup walnut pieces
SAUCE:
1 tablespoon butter
1 tablespoon all-purpose flour
1¼ cups skim milk
¾ cup grated Gruyere cheese
freshly ground black pepper to taste
1 large egg, beaten

Preheat the oven to 375F (190C). Make the dough mixing in the tomato paste with the egg yolk. Cover with plastic wrap and chill for 15 minutes. Heat the oil in a small skillet. Add the leeks and crush the garlic cloves into the pan. Gently sauté until the leeks are softened. Add the butter, flour, and milk to a saucepan. Whisk over a medium heat until thickened and then add the cheese and pepper. Beat in the egg.

Roll the dough out to ¼-inch thickness and use to line an 8-inch loose-bottomed quiche pan. Trim any excess. Spread the leek and garlic mixture over the bottom. Arrange the asparagus tips in a circle, tips pointing outward, and pour the cheese sauce over the asparagus and bake for 35–40 minutes. Roast the walnut pieces separately until brown and sprinkle over the top.

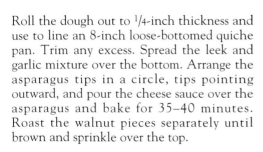

Serves 4

QUICHE LORRAINE

DOUGH:
1 recipe Wholewheat Dough (page 10)
FILLING:
1 tablespoon olive oil
1 medium brown onion, halved and sliced
2 cups sliced button mushrooms
scant 1 cup (4 oz) cubed cooked ham
$^2/_3$ cup grated sharp cheddar cheese
3 large eggs
$^1/_2$ cup skim milk
1 tablespoon chopped fresh parsley or 1 teaspoon
   dried
freshly ground black pepper to taste

Preheat the oven to 350F (180C).

Lightly butter and flour an 8-inch loose-bottomed quiche pan. Make the dough. Cover in plastic wrap and chill for 20 minutes. Roll the dough out to about 9 inches in diameter and using the rolling pin, lift the dough into the pan. Trim away the excess with the rolling pin and cover in plastic wrap and chill for 20 minutes.

Heat the oil in a skillet and cook the onion and mushrooms for about 5 minutes until golden. Drain on a plate lined with paper towels before adding to the pastry shell. Sprinkle the cooked ham over the top, followed by the cheese. Beat the eggs, milk, parsley, and seasoning together and pour over the filling ingredients. Bake for 35–40 minutes until golden brown and the filling has set.

Serves 4–6

- APPLE & BLUE CHEESE QUICHE -

DOUGH:
1 recipe Basic Pie Dough (page 9) adding 1/4 cup
   sour cream
FILLING:
1 large rib celery, thinly sliced
1 medium brown onion, sliced into rings
1 tablespoon canola oil
2 medium eating apples, cored
1 tablespoon lemon juice
2 large eggs, plus a little egg white
1/2 cup skim milk
1 tablespoon chopped fresh thyme
freshly ground black pepper to taste
1 cup crumbled Stilton or similar blue cheese

Preheat the oven to 375F (190C). Prepare
the dough adding the sour cream with the
egg yolk. Cover the dough with plastic wrap
and chill for 15 minutes. Heat the oil in a
small skillet and sauté the celery and onion
for 5 minutes. Cut the apples into 1/2-inch
slices and sprinkle with lemon juice. Blend
the eggs, milk, thyme, and pepper together.

Roll the dough out to 1/4-inch thickness and
line an 8-inch loose-bottomed quiche pan.
Trim away excess with a rolling pin. Prick
the bottom with a fork and brush with a
little egg white. Bake blind for 10 minutes.
Add the celery and onion to the bottom and
sprinkle the blue cheese over the top. Pour
in the egg mixture and top with the apple
slices. Bake for 30–35 minutes until golden
brown and the filling has set.

Serves 4

──── THREE-HERBED SOUFFLE ────

DOUGH:
1 can ready-made croissant dough
$^1/_4$ cup egg wash
FILLING:
1 tablespoon each of basil, mint, and chervil
2 large eggs, separated
1 cup light cream
1 cup finely grated Monterey Jack cheese

Preheat the oven to 375F (190C). Finely chop the herbs. Using a whisk, beat the egg yolks and cream together in a heatproof bowl placed over a pan of gently simmering water, until slightly thickened. Mix in the herbs and cheese. Whisk the egg whites until stiff and gently fold into the cream mixture.

To make the crust, open the croissant can and separate the triangles of dough. Use three triangles to line the bottom of an 8-inch quiche pan and cut the fourth triangle to fit any gaps. Press where the edges of the croissant dough meet to seal the gaps. Brush the bottom and sides with the egg wash. Add the filling and bake for 25–30 minutes until golden brown. Serve immediately.

Serves 4

GOAT CHEESE QUICHE

DOUGH:
1/2 recipe Basic Pie Dough (page 9)
1 recipe Cream Puff Dough (page 11)
FILLING:
1 medium red onion, finely chopped
2 garlic cloves, peeled and crushed
1 tablespoon olive oil
1 1/2 cups soft goat cheese
10 slices pancetta, roughly chopped
2 tablespoons chopped basil
freshly ground black pepper to taste
1/4 cup red pesto sauce
1/4 cup grated Emmenthal or Swiss cheese

Preheat oven to 375F (190C).

Make the dough, cover in plastic wrap, and chill for 15 minutes. Heat the oil and sauté the onion and garlic until soft. Blend the cheese, pancetta, basil, and pepper. Roll the dough out to 1/8 inch thick and line an 8-inch loose-based, 2-inch deep quiche pan. Trim off excess. Bake blind for 5 minutes. Remove waxed paper and pie weights and bake for another 8 minutes. Make the Cream Puff Dough and spoon into a pastry bag fitted with a large plain tip. Pipe twelve 2-inch balls onto a baking sheet.

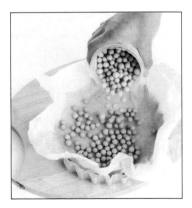

Turn the oven up to 400F (200C). Bake the cream puff balls for about 12–15 minutes until risen and golden. Make a small cut in the bottom of each ball. Spoon a little of the goat cheese mixture into each puff through the cut. Spread the bottom of each cream puff with pesto sauce and top with the onion and garlic. Place the filled cream puffs on top of the onion and sprinkle over the grated cheese. Bake for 10 minutes to warm through.

Serves 4

— SUN-DRIED TOMATO QUICHE —

DOUGH:
6 tablespoons butter, cubed
1 cup plus 3 tablespoons self-rising flour
3 tablespoons wholewheat flour
2 large egg yolks, reserve the whites
1/3 cup chilled water to mix
FILLING:
12 oz lean boneless lamb
8 sun-dried tomatoes (in oil)
1 tablespoon olive oil
1 medium brown onion, roughly chopped
2 large eggs, plus reserved whites (from dough)
1 cup plain yogurt
freshly ground black pepper to taste
2 tablespoons green pesto sauce
1/3 cup grated Pecorino cheese

Preheat oven to 375F (190C). Cut the butter into the flours. Mix in the egg yolks and enough water to bind the mixture together to form a soft dough. Cover with plastic wrap and chill for 20 minutes. Dice the tomatoes and cut the lamb into strips. Heat the oil in a skillet, add the onion and cook for 2–3 minutes. Add the lamb and cook until browned. Blend the eggs into the yogurt and season. Whisk the egg whites until stiff and gently fold into the mixture.

Roll the dough out to 1/4-inch thickness onto a lightly floured surface, and use to line a 9-inch quiche pan. Trim the edges. Spread the pesto over the bottom of the pastry and add the onion and lamb. Pour the egg mixture over the top and sprinkle the grated cheese over to finish. Bake for 30–35 minutes until golden.

Serves 4–6

TUSCAN TART

PASTRY:
6 sheets phyllo pastry, 15 x 11-inches
2 tablespoons melted butter
FILLING:
2 (8-oz) smoked haddock fillets
1/2 cup 2% milk
2 tablespoons chopped fresh dill
1 bay leaf
1 cup fresh peas, shelled
1 cup sour cream
2 large eggs
freshly ground black pepper to taste
1/3 cup dry white wine

Preheat oven to 375F (190C). Place the fish in a shallow ovenproof dish and add the milk and bay leaf. Cover with aluminum foil and bake for 15–20 minutes until cooked. Remove the fish, reserving the milk, and flake into a bowl. Bring a small pan of slightly salted water to a boil and cook the peas for 2–3 minutes. Drain. Strain the reserved milk into another bowl and add the peas, chopped dill, and sour cream. Beat in the eggs and pepper. Mix in the flaked haddock and wine.

Lay the sheets of phyllo on a lightly floured surface and brush with the melted butter. Fold in half and lay them into a buttered 8-inch quiche pan. Overlap the sheets by half, leaving 1 inch of the pastry hanging over the edge. Brush with more butter and add the filling. Bake for 25–30 minutes until the pastry is golden and the filling is set.

Serves 4

PORK & APRICOT QUICHE

DOUGH:
1 recipe Basic Pie Dough (page 9)
FILLING:
1 head of fennel
1 tablespoon canola oil
14 oz pork tenderloin, 1-inch cubed
1/4 cup raisins
2 tablespoons onion relish
1/3 cup dried apricots, roughly chopped
1/2 cup sour cream
3 large eggs
1 tablespoon chopped fresh sage
freshly ground black pepper to taste
arugula leaves to garnish

Preheat the oven to 375F (190C). Make the dough. Cover in plastic wrap and chill for 15 minutes. Roll out to a 1/4 inch thickness and line a 9-inch quiche dish. Cut the fennel in half, remove the tough center, and then roughly chop. Heat the oil in a skillet and add the meat. Cook for 10 minutes over a gentle heat then add the fennel. Continue cooking for 5 minutes.

Bake the pastry case blind for 10 minutes. Add the raisins to the relish and spread over the bottom of the pastry. Add the pork, fennel, and apricots. Blend the sour cream, eggs, and sage together and season. Pour over the filling ingredients and bake for 40–45 minutes, covering with aluminum foil mid-way if the top starts to brown too quickly. Garnish with a few arugula leaves or serve with a arugula salad.

Serves 4–6

SUNFLOWER SEED & OAT QUICHE

DOUGH:
1/4 cup sunflower seeds
scant 1/2 cup rolled oats
1 cup all-purpose flour
6 tablespoons butter, cubed
1 large egg yolk
1/3 cup chilled water to mix
FILLING:
1/3 cup soft goat cheese
1/3 cup chopped dried apricots
1/2 cup light cream
2 large eggs, beaten
1 tablespoon fresh chopped thyme
1 tablespoon slivered almonds, toasted

Preheat oven to 375F (190C). In a small pan, toast the sunflower seeds over a gentle heat until browned. Place these, the oats, flour, and butter into a food processor and blend together. Add the egg yolk and enough cold water to form a soft dough. Cover with plastic wrap and chill for 20 minutes. Roll the dough out to a 1/8-inch thickness and carefully lift into an 8-inch quiche pan with the rolling pin. Repair any gaps by pressing a little of the trimmings into the spaces.

Crumble the goat cheese into the bottom of the pastry shell. Blend the remaining filling ingredients together and pour over the cheese. Bake for 25–30 minutes. Top with slivers of almonds after baking.

Serves 4

— ARTICHOKE & PATE QUICHE —

DOUGH:
6 tablespoons butter, cubed
1 1/2 cups all-purpose flour
6 sun-dried tomatoes (in oil), finely chopped
1 tablespoon roughly chopped fresh basil
1 large egg yolk
1/4 cup chilled water to mix
FILLING:
1 (14-oz) can artichoke hearts, drained
6 oz coarse liver pâté
1 cup sour cream
1/4 cup light cream
3 large egg yolks, plus 2 whites
8 cherry tomatoes, sliced
freshly ground black pepper to taste

Preheat the oven to 375F (190C). Cut the butter into the flour and add the tomatoes, basil, and egg yolk. Add enough cold water to bind the ingredients together to form a soft dough. Cover in plastic wrap and chill for 20 minutes. Roughly chop the artichokes and cube the liver pâté. In a bowl, blend the sour cream, cream, yolks and egg whites, reserving 1 tablespoon of egg white, and season.

Roll out the dough to a 1/4-inch thickness and line a 9-inch quiche dish. Brush the pastry with the reserved egg white and bake blind for 10 minutes before adding the artichoke pieces and pâté. Pour the cream mixture over the top and decorate with tomato slices. Bake for 30–40 minutes until lightly browned and the filling is set. Cover with aluminum foil if it browns too quickly.

Serves 4–6

EMPANADAS

DOUGH:
1²/₃ cups all-purpose flour
1 teaspoon paprika
¹/₂ cup butter, cubed
1 large egg yolk
¹/₄ cup chilled water to mix
1 tablespoon egg wash
FILLING:
1 lb lean ground beef
¹/₃ cup golden raisins
1 red chili, seeded, finely chopped
1 green chili, seeded, finely chopped
1 cup canned tomato sauce with garlic and herbs
1 teaspoon Cajun seasoning
freshly ground black pepper to taste

Preheat the oven to 375F (190C). Place the flour and paprika into a food processor and add the butter. Blend using a pulse action; add the egg yolk and enough cold water to bind the mixture. Remove from processor and cover with plastic wrap. Chill for 15 minutes. Heat a nonstick skillet, stirring for 5 minutes until browned. Remove with a slotted spoon, leaving the fat in the skillet, and place on a paper towel to drain. Place raisins and chilies in a bowl. Add the meat, tomato sauce, and seasoning.

Roll the dough out to a ¹/₈-inch thickness and cut out eight 6-inch rounds, using a similar sized saucer as a guide. Brush the edges of the circles with egg wash and place a tablespoon of the meat filling onto one half. Fold the other half over the filling and seal the edges with the flat side of a sharp knife. Cut two small slits in the top of the crescent shapes and place on a baking sheet, ¹/₂ inch apart. Brush with egg wash and bake for 10–15 minutes until crisp.

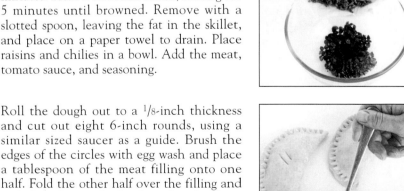

Makes 8

— SAUSAGE & TOMATO BRAID —

DOUGH:
1 recipe Basic Flaky Pie Dough (page 10) but use 2
   cups flour and 1 cup butter (or use 10 oz ready-
   made puff pastry)
1 tablespoon egg wash
FILLING:
6 large pork and beef sausages or 14 oz sausage meat
2 tablespoons freshly chopped mixed herbs (e.g.
   parsley and sage)
1 tablespoon prepared mustard (any)
salt and freshly ground black pepper to taste
4 small tomatoes, sliced

Preheat the oven to 400F (200C). If using
sausages, remove from their skins by cutting
along their length, then peeling away the
skin, and place in a bowl. Add the herbs,
mustard, and seasoning and mix well. Roll
out dough (on a heavily floured surface if
using Flaky pastry or lightly floured if using
Puff) to create a 12 x 10-inch rectangle, 1/4
inch thick. Make 2-inch deep diagonal cuts
along the length of the pastry from the
outside right and left hand edges. Spoon the
filling into the center of the pastry and egg-
wash the edges.

Lay the tomato slices on top of the sausage
meat and fold the top and bottom end up
over the filling. Starting from one end, lay
alternate strips over each other to make a
"braid" pattern. Cut out a few stars of excess
dough to decorate the top. Brush some egg
wash over the top and bake for 35–40
minutes. Cover with foil if the braid starts
to brown too quickly.

Serves 4–6

RATATOUILLE PARCELS

DOUGH:
1 recipe Basic Pie Dough (page 9)
1 tablespoon egg wash
1 tablespoon grated Parmesan
FILLING:
1 tablespoon olive oil
6 oz eggplant, diced
1 small zucchini, diced
1/2 large red bell pepper, seeded and diced
4 small tomatoes (8 oz), roughly chopped
10 pitted black olives, roughly chopped
1 tablespoon fresh parsley, chopped
salt and freshly ground black pepper to taste

Preheat the oven to 375F (190C). Make the dough, cover in plastic wrap and chill for 15 minutes. Meanwhile heat the oil in a large skillet and add the eggplant, zucchini, pepper, and tomatoes. Cook for 5 minutes until softened. Add the chopped olives and parsley and season to taste. Allow to cool. Divide the dough into quarters and roll each piece out to a 1/4-inch thickness and cut out four 6 1/2-inch diameter circles using a crimper wheel.

Brush the egg wash around the edges and place a heaped tablespoon of the ratatouille mixture into the center of each circle. Bring the edges together and press to seal. Flute the edges (page 9) and place on a lightly greased baking sheet. Brush with egg wash and sprinkle with a little Parmesan cheese. Bake for 15–20 minutes until crisp and golden brown. Serve with a dressed salad.

Makes 4

— HAM & EGG PASTRY BALLS —

DOUGH:
1 recipe Basic Hot Water Dough (page 11)
FILLING:
4 large eggs, room temperature
6 Lincolnshire Sausages or 14 oz coarsely chopped
  lean pork and sage sausage meat
6 sprigs fresh thyme, chopped
1 cup sharp cheddar, coarsely grated
freshly ground black pepper to taste
8 oz cucumber, seeded

Preheat the oven to 375F (190C). Bring a pan of water to a boil and carefully lower the eggs into the water to prevent cracking. Simmer for 6 minutes, then drain.

When cool enough to handle remove the shells. Cut a slit down the length of the sausage skins and remove. Place sausage meat into a bowl and add the thyme. Add the cheese to the bowl and mix well. Take a quarter of the sausage mixture and flatten slightly in the palm of your hand. Put a boiled egg in the center and gently mold the sausage meat around it to enclose it completely.

Divide the dough into quarters and roll out four 5-inch diameter circles, to a 1/4-inch thickness. Place an egg on each circle and encase the sausage meat with the dough. Trim away any excess dough. Place on a baking sheet. Brush with egg wash and cut some small leaves from the dough trimmings for decoration (page 9). Bake for 25–30 minutes until golden and cooked. Cut the cucumber into 1/2-inch batons and serve with the pastry balls.

Makes 4

CALZONE

DOUGH:
$^1/_2$ tablespoon butter
1$^3/_4$ cups strong bread flour
pinch of caster sugar
1 teaspoon dried oregano
1 teaspoon instant yeast
$^1/_2$ cup warm skim milk
pinch of salt
1 tablespoon egg wash
$^1/_3$ cup freshly grated Parmesan cheese
FILLING:
14 oz lean ground beef
1 medium onion, finely chopped
1 small red bell pepper, boiled, peeled, and roughly
    chopped (see page 81)
1 cup tomato sauce

1$^1/_3$ cups cubed mozzarella
8–10 large basil leaves, roughly torn
freshly ground black pepper to taste

Preheat the oven to 400F (200C). Cut the butter into the flour and stir in the sugar, salt, oregano, and yeast. Gradually add the milk to form a soft dough. Turn out onto a lightly floured surface and knead lightly. Place in a lightly oiled bowl, cover, and leave in a warm place until it has doubled in size. Cook the ground beef in a large skillet until just browned. Add onion and pepper.

Cook for another 2 minutes and add the sauce, mozzarella, and basil. Mix well and season. Divide the dough into quarters and roll out to 8-inch diameter circles $^1/_2$ inch thick. Brush around the edges with egg wash. Place $^1/_4$ of the meat sauce onto one half of each circle and fold the other half over the meat. Press down to seal the edges. Place on a baking sheet, brush with egg wash, and sprinkle with the grated Parmesan. Bake for 25–30 minutes.

Makes 4

DIJON PORK EN CROUTE

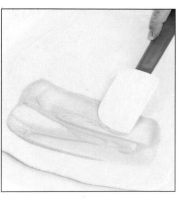

PASTRY:
10 oz ready-made puff pastry
1 tablespoon egg wash
FILLING:
1 lb pork tenderloin
2 tablespoons brandy or cognac
juice and zest of 1 large orange
1/2 tablespoon butter
4 oz baby brown mushrooms, cleaned
2 tablespoons Dijon mustard
1 tablespoon sour cream
1 tablespoon freshly chopped sage
freshly ground black pepper to taste

Preheat the oven to 375F (190C). Cut the pork into 1/2-inch strips and place in a bowl along with the brandy, orange juice, and zest. Mix well and leave to marinate for 1 hour. Melt the butter in a skillet and cook the mushrooms for 2–3 minutes. Blend the mustard and sour cream together. On a lightly floured board, roll the dough out to make a large rectangle, 12 x 10-inches, 1/4 inch thick. Spread the mustard and sour cream over the pastry leaving a 2-inch border all the way around and brush the edges with egg wash.

Remove the pork strips, discarding the liquid, and put them down the center of the pastry leaving a 2-inch border all round. Lay the mushrooms on top, along with the chopped sage. Fold the ends of the pastry over the filling and then fold in the sides to completely encase the filling. Lay the pastry, folded side down, onto a baking sheet, decorate with pastry trimmings and brush with egg wash. Bake for 25–30 minutes until golden brown.

Serves 4

VEGETABLE TURNOVERS

DOUGH:
1 recipe Flaky Pie Dough (page 10)
1 tablespoon egg wash
1 tablespoon poppy seeds
FILLING:
4 oz waxy potatoes, diced
3 oz carrots, diced
2 oz asparagus tips, chopped
2 oz broccoli, cut into florets
SAUCE:
1 tablespoon butter
1 tablespoon all-purpose flour
1 cup skim milk
1/3 cup grated sharp cheddar cheese
freshly ground black pepper to taste

Preheat the oven to 400F (200C). Make the dough, cover in plastic wrap, and chill for 1 hour. Add the butter, flour, and milk to a small saucepan and whisk over a medium heat. Simmer for 2–3 minutes, add the cheese, and season. Blanch the vegetables and add to the cheese sauce. Cool.

Roll the dough out onto a heavily floured surface to a 1/4-inch thickness. Cut out four 7-inch squares of dough and brush egg wash over the edges. Place a quarter of the vegetable filling on one side of each square and fold the other side over to make a triangle. Flute the edges (page 9) and press to seal. Place on a baking sheet and brush with egg wash. Sprinkle with poppy seeds and bake for 15–20 minutes until risen and golden brown.

Makes 4

— PISTACHIO PHYLLO WRAPS —

PASTRY:
6 sheets phyllo, 15 x 11-inches
2 tablespoons melted butter
12 fresh chives to garnish
FILLING:
1 cup (3 oz) crumbled Stilton (or equivalent blue cheese)
1 oz dates, pitted
1 oz pistachio nuts, shelled
1 tablespoon chopped thyme
freshly ground black pepper to taste

Preheat oven to 375F (190C). Place the Stilton into a small bowl. Finely chop the dates and pistachio nuts. Mix into the cheese and season. Cut the phyllo sheets in half, across the width. (Keep the pastry covered with plastic wrap while you make the wraps to prevent it drying out.) Brush each half with melted butter and fold in half again.

Place a teaspoon of mixture into the center of the phyllo rectangle and pinch the surrounding pastry together over the filling to seal, pressing the center quite firmly to hold the wrap together. Place on baking sheet, brush with a little butter, and bake for 10–15 minutes until golden brown. Tie a chive stalk around the middle of each wrap and serve.

Makes 12

FOLDED CHINESE PARCELS

PASTRY:
13 sheets phyllo, 15 x 11-inches
2 tablespoons melted butter
FILLING:
1 lb skinless, boneless chicken breasts
1 tablespoon peanut oil
grated zest and juice of 1 lemon
1-inch piece fresh ginger, peeled and thinly sliced
1/4 cup pineapple juice
1 large carrot, peeled
1 oz bamboo shoots
1 oz bean sprouts
1 teaspoon cornstarch
1 tablespoon water
freshly ground black pepper to taste

Preheat the oven to 375F (190C). Cut the chicken into 1/2-inch thick strips. Heat the oil in a wok over a medium heat until just smoking and add the chicken. Cook for 5 minutes until the chicken is no longer pink. Thinly slice the carrot and bamboo shoots. In a smaller skillet heat the lemon zest, lemon juice, and pineapple juice for 1 minute before adding the carrot, bamboo shoots, and sprouts. Heat for an additional minute then add the cornstarch, blended with water, and stir until slightly thickened.

Add to the wok and stir well. Lay a sheet of phyllo on a flat surface and brush with melted butter. Fold in half crosswise and brush with butter again. Place a small mound of filling onto the center of the phyllo and make a parcel. Wrap again with another sheet. Use the last sheet to make small decorations for the top of the parcels. Brush with a little more butter and place on a baking sheet. Bake for 15–20 minutes until golden brown and crisp.

Makes 6

INDIAN ROTI ROLLS

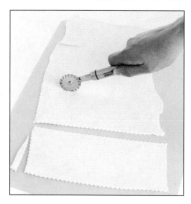

PASTRY:
10 oz ready-made puff pastry
1 tablespoon egg wash
1 teaspoon poppy seeds
FILLING:
1 teaspoon madras curry paste
1/4 cup chicken broth
1 cup (6 oz) cooked skinless, boneless chicken
  breast, diced
1 green bell pepper, seeded and chopped
1/4 cup unflavored yogurt
1 teaspoon freshly chopped cilantro
freshly ground black pepper to taste
RAITA:
1/2 cup Greek style yogurt
1 teaspoon fresh lime juice

1/4 cucumber (4 oz), peeled, seeded, and finely
  chopped
8 fresh mint leaves, roughly chopped

Preheat the oven to 375F (190C). Roll the
pastry out to a 1/4-inch thickness and cut out
four small rectangles, 7 x 3-inches wide,
using a pastry wheel. Brush some egg wash
around the edges of the rectangles. In a
small bowl blend the curry paste with the
broth and pour over the chicken and pepper
in a small saucepan.

Stir in the unflavored yogurt and cilantro,
and pepper. Bring to a gentle simmer for 5
minutes. Place a quarter of the mixture on
one side of each rectangle and fold the other
half over the filling. Seal the edges together
using the pastry wheel. Brush the top with
egg wash, sprinkle with poppy seeds, and
bake for 10–15 minutes until golden brown.
Mix all the ingredients together for the
Raita and serve with the rolls.

Makes 4

BOREK

PASTRY:
8 sheets phyllo pastry, 15 x 11-inches
2 tablespoons butter, melted
FILLING:
1 tablespoon coriander seeds
4 cardamon pods, split open
12 peppercorns
2 blades of mace (or ½ teaspoon ground nutmeg)
pinch sea salt flakes
1 teaspoon cayenne pepper
10 oz lean boneless lamb
2 cloves garlic, peeled and crushed
1 tablespoon sunflower or canola oil
1 small onion, roughly chopped

Preheat the oven to 375F (190C). Place all of the spices and salt into a pestle and mortar and grind to a fine powder. Cut the lamb into small cubes, trimming away the fat, and place in a mixing bowl. Add the ground spices and garlic. Mix well. Heat the oil in a skillet over a medium heat and cook the onion for 2 minutes until soft. Add the spiced lamb mixture, turn down the heat, cover, and cook for 15 minutes, stirring occasionally.

Lay the phyllo sheets, one at a time, on a surface and brush with melted butter. Fold in half and place a tablespoon of the cooled spiced lamb onto one end, (leaving a ½-inch gap from the end of the sheet). Turn the end of the pastry over the filling and fold in the sides. Roll up like a spring roll, brushing with melted butter. Place on a baking sheet and bake for 10–15 minutes until golden.

Makes 8

HONEYED DUCK RINGS

DOUGH:
1 recipe Basic Pie Dough (page 9) replacing 4
   tablespoons of the butter with cream cheese and
   herbs
6 sage leaves, roughly chopped
1/4 cup egg wash
FILLING:
2 skinless duck breasts
1/2 tablespoon butter (clarified)
2 teaspoons cornstarch
zest and juice of 1 large orange plus 1 cup fresh
   orange juice
1 tablespoon clover honey
freshly ground black pepper to taste

Preheat the oven to 375F (190C). Make the
dough adding the cream cheese with herbs
after the butter has been cut into the flour.
Cover the dough with plastic wrap and chill
for 15 minutes. Cut the duck into thin
slices, diagonally across the grain of the
meat. Melt the butter in a small skillet and
flash fry the duck for 2 minutes. Remove
from the heat. Roll the dough out to a 1/8-
inch thickness. Using a 4^{1}/2-inch fluted
cutter, cut out eight circles. Using a 2-inch
fluted cutter, cut out smaller circles from the
center of four of the dough circles.

Place the four whole circles on a baking
sheet, brush egg wash around the edges, and
arrange duck slices on top. Blend the cornstarch with a little orange juice to make a
smooth paste. Add the remaining juice, zest,
and honey to a saucepan. Stir in the paste
and heat, stirring until thickened. Season.
Spoon sauce over the duck. Top with the
pastry rings, pressing edges to seal. Brush
with egg wash. Bake for 15 minutes until
golden.

Makes 4

— CURRIED CHICKEN SQUARES —

DOUGH:
2 cups self-rising flour
6 tablespoons butter, cubed
$^1/_2$ teaspoon turmeric
$^1/_2$ teaspoon cumin
$^1/_4$ cup soured cream
$^1/_4$ cup chilled water to mix
$^1/_4$ cup egg wash
FILLING:
1 oz creamed coconut
$^1/_4$ cup hot water
1 tablespoon mild curry paste
$^1/_3$ cup plain yogurt
1 tablespoon chopped fresh cilantro
freshly ground black pepper to taste
2 skinless, boneless chicken breasts, cubed

Preheat the oven to 375F (190C). Blend the creamed coconut into the hot water and stir in the curry paste, yogurt, and herbs. Add the chicken and mix well. Place in the refrigerator and leave to marinate for 20 minutes. For the dough, sift the flour into a mixing bowl and cut the butter in until it resembles breadcrumbs. Stir in the turmeric and cumin. Add the soured cream and enough cold water (about $^1/_3$ cup) to bind the mixture together to form a soft dough. Cover with plastic wrap. Chill for 20 minutes.

On a lightly floured surface roll the dough out into a large rectangle, $^1/_8$ inch thick, and cut out 16 squares of dough, about $3^1/_2$ x $3^1/_2$ inches. Brush some egg wash around the edges of eight of the squares and place small mounds of the mixture in the center of each. Using a lattice pastry roller, roll over the remaining squares to create a patterned lid. Press around the edges to seal. Place on a baking sheet, brush the tops with egg wash, and bake for 15–20 minutes.

Makes 8

— SMOKED MACKEREL DELIGHTS —

PASTRY:
6 sheets phyllo, 15 x 11-inches
2 tablespoons melted butter
1 tablespoon sesame seeds
2 scallions, trimmed
thin red onion slices to garnish
lemon wedges to garnish
FILLING:
8 oz smoked mackerel fillets
6 oz cream cheese with garlic and herbs
grated zest and juice of ½ lemon
freshly ground black pepper to taste

Preheat the oven to 375F (190C). Remove the skins from the mackerel and flake the fish into a bowl. Add the cream cheese, lemon zest, and juice. Mix well and season. Cut the phyllo sheets in half, across the width, and brush with melted butter. Place a teaspoon of filling at one end of the rectangle and roll the phyllo up to make a sausage shape. Pinch the phyllo together at either side of the filling to create a cracker shape. Brush with butter, sprinkle with sesame seeds, and place on a baking sheet.

Bake for 10 minutes until golden then garnish with the scallions, red onion slices, and lemon wedges.

Makes 12

NOTE: To make the garnish cut a trimmed scallion in half crosswise. Hold one end and with a sharp knife make a cut from the center to the end. Turn the scallion and repeat the cut three times. Take care not to cut any strips off. Leave in a bowl of iced water for 20 minutes until they have curled.

CHIMCHANGAS

DOUGH:
½ cup plus 1 tablespoon fine cornmeal
1 cup all-purpose flour
½ cup butter
1 large egg yolk
¼ cup water
FILLING:
4 scallions, trimmed
2 cups smoked or Provolone cheese, cubed
1 red chili, seeded and finely chopped
1 green chili, seeded and finely chopped
5 cups vegetable oil for deep-frying
SALSA:
2 Hass or Fuerte avocados
1 lime
2 large tomatoes, seeded and diced

1 cucumber, peeled and diced
1 tablespoon freshly chopped cilantro
freshly ground black pepper to taste

Put the cornmeal and the flour into a food processor. Add the butter and use the pulse action to blend. Add yolk and enough water to bind. Cover the dough with plastic wrap and chill for 15 minutes. For the salsa, remove seeds from the avocados and dice flesh. Transfer to a bowl and squeeze the juice of half the lime over it for flavor and to prevent the avocados from browning.

Mix the tomatoes, cucumber, and cilantro in a bowl. Squeeze the other lime half over, season, and mix well. Roll the dough out to a ⅛-inch thickness and cut out 10 rectangles 5 x 6-inches. Brush edges with water and place a tablespoon of the mixture on one side. Fold the other half over and press edges to seal. Heat the oil to 375F (190C). Deep-fry for 5–6 minutes until crisp and golden. Drain on paper towels. Serve with the salsa.

Makes 10

— CHICKEN & CUMIN PASTIES —

DOUGH:
single quantity of Wholewheat Pie Dough (page 10)
1/2 teaspoon each of turmeric and paprika
1/4 cup egg wash
FILLING:
2 small skinless, boneless chicken breasts, diced
1 teaspoon canola oil
2 teaspoons cumin seeds
1/2 small cauliflower, cut into small florets
2 oz snow peas, destringed, cleaned, and cut into thirds
1/4 cup chicken broth
freshly ground black pepper to taste

Preheat the oven to 375F (190C). When making the dough stir in the turmeric and paprika before adding the egg yolk and water To make filling: heat the oil in a skillet over a medium heat and add the chicken. Cook for 3–4 minutes and add the cumin seeds. Cook for 2 minutes and remove from the heat. Steam the cauliflower florets for 5 minutes—they should still be slightly firm when a knife tip is inserted into them. Add them to the chicken, along with the snow peas and broth, and season. Allow to cool.

On a lightly floured surface, roll the dough out to a 1/4-inch thickness and cut eight 4-inch round disks using a saucer, plain cutter or pastry wheel. Brush the edges with egg wash and place a small mound of filling (about 2 teaspoons) on one side. Fold the other side up and over the filling and press the edges together. Crimp edges. Place on a baking sheet, brush with egg wash, and bake for 15–20 minutes until the pastry is cooked and crisp.

Makes 8

PUMPKIN TART

DOUGH:
1 recipe Basic Pie Dough (page 9) but use an extra
 1/3 cup all-purpose flour and 2 tablespoons butter
FILLING:
1 stalk lemongrass
1 bouquet garni
10 oz fresh pumpkin chunks
1/3 cup light cream
1/2-inch piece fresh ginger, peeled
3 large eggs
1/2 cup 2% milk
2 teaspoons caraway seeds

Preheat the oven to 375F (190C).

Cut the lemongrass stick into quarters and place in the bottom of a steamer with the bouquet garni and 2¹/₄ cups of water. Place the pumpkin chunks in the top part of the steamer and cook for 15 minutes until soft. Transfer to a bowl and mash slightly, leaving a few chunks for texture. Add the cream and grate the ginger into the bowl. Beat in the eggs and milk. Roll the dough out to a ¹/₈-inch thickness and line a 10-inch loose-bottomed shallow tart pan.

Bake blind with a piece of waxed paper and baking beans for 10 minutes, then remove these and bake for a further 5 minutes. Place the tart pan on a baking sheet and pour in the filling. Sprinkle the caraway seeds over the top and bake for 45 minutes until golden and set.

Serves 6–8

— LEEK & GOAT CHEESE TART —

DOUGH:
1 cup plus 2 tablespoons all-purpose flour
5 tablespoons butter
1 tablespoon sun-dried tomatoes (in oil), chopped
1 egg yolk
1/4 cup chilled water to mix
FILLING:
2 tablespoons butter
1 small red onion, chopped
5 oz baby leeks, washed
1/4 cup 2% milk
1/4 cup sour cream
2 large eggs
freshly ground black pepper to taste
1 1/2 cups (5 oz) soft goat cheese
1/3 cup Double Gloucester cheese or yellow mild
    cheddar, finely grated

Preheat oven to 375F (190C). Blend the butter into the flour and add the tomatoes, egg yolk, and enough water to bind the ingredients together. Cover in plastic wrap and chill for 15 minutes. Thinly slice the leeks. In a small skillet, melt the butter over a medium heat. Add the onion and leeks and cook for 2–3 minutes. Blend the milk, sour cream, and eggs together and season.

Roll out the dough to a 1/4-inch thickness and line the tart tin. Trim the edges with the rolling pin. Prick the bottom of the pastry and bake blind, without waxed paper or pie weights, for 10 minutes Spoon the vegetables into the tart shell and crumble the goat cheese over the top. Pour the milk mixture over this and sprinkle the grated cheese over the surface. Bake for 30–35 minutes.

Serves 4–6

ROASTED PEPPER TART

DOUGH:
1 cup all-purpose flour
2 oz cream cheese with herbs
1 teaspoon Mediterranean dried herbs
 (oregano/basil/parsley)
1 large egg yolk (reserve the white)
$^{1}/_{4}$ cup chilled water to mix
FILLING:
1 red bell pepper, seeded and quartered
1 green bell pepper, seeded and quartered
1 yellow bell pepper, seeded and quartered
$1^{1}/_{3}$ cups soft goat cheese
$^{1}/_{3}$ cup 2% milk
2 large eggs
freshly ground black pepper to taste

Preheat oven to 375F (190C). Preheat the broiler to a high temperature and cook the peppers for about 5 minutes until the skins start to blister and turn black. Allow to cool in a plastic food bag or container with a lid and then remove the skins. Cut into thin strips. Sift the flour into a bowl and mix in the cream cheese with the blade of a rounded knife or a palette knife. Mix in the herbs. Add the egg yolk and enough cold water to bind. Cover with plastic wrap and chill for 20 minutes.

Roll the dough out to a $^{1}/_{8}$-inch thickness and line the bottom of an 8-inch loose-bottomed tart pan. Brush the bottom with a little of the reserved egg white and then whisk the remainder to a soft foam. Blend the goat cheese, milk, and eggs together. Season and gently fold in the rest of the egg white. Arrange the pepper strips in bands of one color across the bottom and pour the filling mixture over the top. Bake for 30–35 minutes until golden and the filling has set.

Serves 4

SPANISH FLAN

DOUGH:
1 recipe Rough Puff Dough (page 10) adding 1
  tablespoon of chopped fresh basil to the flour
FILING:
1 tablespoon olive oil
1 medium red onion, halved and sliced
3 medium tomatoes
6 oz spicy chorizo pork sausage
6 oz soft sheep cheese
2 eggs, separated
1/3 cup skim milk
freshly ground black pepper to taste

Preheat the oven to 400F (200C). Make the
dough and chill for 1 hour, covered in
plastic wrap. Heat the oil in a small skillet
and sauté the onion until just beginning to
brown around the edges. Transfer to a plate
lined with paper towel. Thinly slice the
tomatoes and then dice the chorizo. Blend
the sheep cheese, egg yolks, and milk
together and season. Roll the dough out to a
1/4-inch thickness and use it to line the
bottom of an 8-inch loose-bottomed shallow
tart pan. Trim any excess with a rolling pin.

Brush the bottom of the pastry with a little
of the egg white and bake blind for 10
minutes. Whisk the remaining egg white to
a stiff foam. Gently fold into the cheese and
milk mixture. Add the onion and diced
chorizo to the bottom. Pour the cheese
filling in and top with the tomato slices.
Bake for 30–35 minutes until golden and set.

Serves 4

NOTE: if the quiche starts to brown too
quickly cover with aluminum foil.

PISSALADIERE

DOUGH:
1 recipe Enriched Pie Dough (page 10)
FILLING:
1 tablespoon olive oil
1 medium red onion, halved and sliced
1 cup tomato sauce with garlic and herbs
1 tablespoon roughly torn basil
1 small jar or can anchovies in oil (10–14 fish)
12 pitted black olives, halved

Preheat oven to 375F (190C). Make the dough, cover in plastic wrap and chill for 20 minutes. Roll the dough out to a ¼-inch thickness and line the bottom of an 8-inch loose-bottomed tart pan. Bake blind for 10 minutes. Remove the waxed paper and pie weights and cook for an additional 8 minutes. Heat the oil in a small skillet and sauté the onion for 5 minutes until just beginning to brown.

Add to the tomato sauce along with the basil. Pour into the baked pie crust. Arrange the anchovies in a lattice pattern over the top of the sauce and place the olive halves in the spaces between. Bake for 15 minutes before serving. Garnish with basil leaves.

Serves 4

NOTE: if using salted anchovies, they can be soaked in milk for a few minutes before using to reduce saltiness.

ALMOND & PEAR TART

DOUGH:
1 recipe Enriched Pie Dough (page 10) replacing
  generous ¹/₄ cup of the flour with ground almonds
FILLING:
1 head fennel
¹/₂ small lemon
2 firm comice pears
1¹/₄ cups light cream
3 large egg yolks, seperated
freshly ground black pepper to taste
1 cup fresh watercress, larger stalks removed
¹/₄ cup walnut halves

Preheat the oven to 375F (190C).

Make the dough, cover with plastic wrap,
and chill for 15 minutes. Cut out the hard
core from the fennel, halve it, and cut into
thin slices. Squeeze a little lemon juice over
it to prevent it browning and give flavor.
Cut the pears in half, remove the core, and
slice the same thickness as the fennel (or a
little thicker as it takes less time to cook).
Pour the cream into a mixing bowl and add
the egg yolks and seasoning. Roll out the
dough to ¹/₈-inch thickness and line the
bottom of a loose-bottomed 9-inch shallow
tart pan.

Using a little of the separated egg white,
brush the pastry bottom, prick, and bake
blind for 10 minutes. Arrange the fennel
and pear slices in the bottom of the pastry
case and sprinkle the watercress over the
top (reserving 3 or 4 sprigs for garnish). Add
the cream and egg mixture and bake for
35–40 minutes. Ten minutes before the end
of the cooking time sprinkle the walnut
pieces onto the surface.

Serves 4–6

TARTE A LA NICOISE

DOUGH:
1 recipe Enriched Pie Dough (page 10)
1 tablespoon freshly chopped basil
FILLING:
1 (10-oz) fresh tuna steak
1 tablespoon butter
10 cherry tomatoes
10 black or green pitted whole olives
¼ cup capers
1 cup tomato paste with herbs
2 large eggs
freshly ground black pepper
6 shredded basil leaves to garnish

Preheat the oven to 375F (190C). Make the dough, adding the chopped basil after cutting the butter into the flour. Cover with plastic wrap and chill for 15 minutes. Preheat a griddle pan over a medium heat. Melt the butter and then add the tuna steak and cook for 2–3 minutes on each side. As soon as the dark pink center of the steak has disappeared remove from the heat. Roll the dough out to a ¼-inch thickness and use it to line a 9-inch loose-bottomed shallow tart pan.

Bake blind for 10 minutes (page 7), then remove the pie weights and waxed paper and bake for an additional 8 minutes. Break the tuna up into large chunks and place in the bottom of the pastry case. Scatter the tomatoes, olives, and capers over the tuna. Beat the eggs into the tomato paste. Pour this over the filling ingredients and bake for 35–40 minutes until set. Sprinkle the basil strips over the tart just before serving.

Serves 4

DUTCH ONION TART

DOUGH:
1 recipe Basic Pie Dough (page 9) adding ⅔ cup
finely grated Edam cheese
FILLING:
1 tablespoon olive oil
4 thick pork and sage sausages
2 medium red onions, halved and sliced
2 medium brown onions, halved and sliced
1 tablespoon brown sugar
1 cup ricotta cheese
2 large eggs
6 sprigs fresh thyme
freshly ground black pepper
⅓ cup grated Edam

Preheat oven to 375F (190C). Make the
dough, cover in plastic wrap, and chill for
15 minutes. Heat the oil in a small skillet
and cook the sausages for 10 minutes,
turning occasionally, until just cooked.
Transfer to some paper towels to drain off
any fat. Slice thickly (6 pieces per sausage).
Add the onions to the skillet and slow cook
for 5–6 minutes. Add the sugar and continue cooking for another 5–6 minutes until
caramelized. In a bowl, blend the ricotta
and eggs together. Pull thyme leaves off
their stems and add to the bowl. Season.

Roll the dough out to a ¼-inch thickness
and use it to line a 9-inch loose-bottomed
tart tin. Trim off any excess with a rolling
pin. Bake blind for 10 minutes then remove
the waxed paper and pie weights and bake
for an additional 8 minutes. Spoon the
onions into the pie crust and add the
sausage pieces. Pour the egg mixture over
the top and finish with the grated cheese.
Bake for 25–30 minutes until golden brown
and set.

Serves 4

CHEESE SOUFFLE TART

DOUGH:
1 recipe Basic Pie Dough (page 9)
1/2 cup cream cheese
FILLING:
1/2 cup cream cheese
2/3 cup blue cheese, crumbled
1/2 cup grated Monterey Jack cheese
2 large eggs, separated into yolks and whites
1/4 cup 2% milk
freshly ground black pepper to taste

Preheat the oven to 375F (190C). Make the dough according to instructions, mixing in the cream cheese after cutting the butter into the flour. Add about 1/4 cup chilled water to the mixture to bind the ingredients together to form a soft dough. Cover with plastic wrap and chill for 15 minutes. Roll the dough out to 1/8-inch thickness and lift it into an 8-inch loose-bottomed deep tart pan. Prick the bottom with a fork and trim away any excess with the rolling pin.

Bake blind with waxed paper and pie weights for 10 minutes and then without for a further 8 minutes. Blend the cheeses, egg yolks, and milk together. Whisk the egg whites until thick and gently fold into the cheese mixture. Pour into the pie crust and bake for 25–30 minutes until risen and golden. Serve immediately.

Serves 4

STUFFED ONION TART

DOUGH:
1 recipe Enriched Pie Dough (page 10)
FILLING:
8–10 large shallots
4 oz cream cheese with herbs
4 thin slices cooked ham
12 basil leaves, finely chopped
freshly ground black pepper to taste
2 cups cherry tomatoes
1 tablespoon olive oil

Preheat the oven to 375F (190C). Make the dough, cover in plastic wrap, and chill for 15 minutes.

Roll out to a ¹/₄-inch thickness and line the bottom of a 14 x 4¹/₂-inch loose-bottomed rectangular tart pan. Bake blind for 10 minutes (page 7). Remove waxed paper and pie weights and return to the oven for 5 minutes. Peel the shallots and trim the ends. Bring a large pan of slightly salted water to a boil and cook the shallots for 5–6 minutes. Transfer to a bowl of cold water for 5 minutes to allow them to cool. Once the shallots are cool enough to handle use a small, sharp paring knife to carefully cut out a small "well" from the center of each.

Discard the centers. Mix the cream cheese, ham, and basil together and season. Using two teaspoons, carefully fill the shallot centers with a little of the filling. Place in the pie crust in a straight line down the middle. Halve the cherry tomatoes crosswise and use to fill the gaps either side of the onions. Drizzle with a little olive oil and bake for 20 minutes.

Serves 4

— BACON & CARAWAY TART —

DOUGH:
1 recipe Basic Pie Dough (page 9)
FILLING:
6 rashers thick, sliced Canadian bacon
2 medium carrots, peeled and trimmed
2 sticks green celery, de-stringed, washed, and
  trimmed
1/2 cup sour cream
1/3 cup skim milk
3 large eggs, beaten
1 tablespoon caraway seeds
1 tablespoon fennel seeds
1/3 cup grated Monterey Jack or any mild cheddar

Preheat the oven to 375F (190C). Using scissors, trim away the bacon rind and cut the bacon slices into small pieces. In a skillet over a medium heat, cook the bacon for 5–6 minutes then transfer to a plate lined with paper towel. Using a wide vegetable peeler cut thin "ribbons" from the length of the carrots. Cut the celery in half and then into thin strips. Blanch the vegetables. Drain on paper towel. Roll the dough out to 1/4-inch thickness and lay in the bottom of a 9-inch loose-bottomed tart pan. Trim any excess with a rolling pin.

Brush the pie crust with a little of the beaten egg (approximately 1 teaspoon) and bake for 5 minutes. Arrange the carrot and celery strips in the bottom of the tart. Blend the sour cream, milk, and remaining eggs together in a bowl and then add the caraway and fennel seeds. Season and mix well. Pour over the vegetables and top with the grated cheese. Bake for 30–35 minutes until golden and set.

Serves 4

— SCRAMBLED EGG TARTLETS —

BOTTOM:
4 slices Irish soda bread
2 tablespoons melted butter
FILLING:
2 oz smoked salmon
$^{1}/_{2}$ lemon
3 large eggs, beaten
$^{1}/_{4}$ cup light cream
1 tablespoon chopped fresh dill or tarragon
freshly ground black pepper to taste

Preheat oven to 375F (190C). Using a 4-inch cutter (plain or fluted) cut four circles out of the soda bread. Lightly flatten with a rolling pin and brush with the melted butter. Place on a baking sheet. Cut the smoked salmon into thin strips and squeeze the lemon juice over them. Place a few strips on the top of each "tartlet" bottom.

Blend the eggs, cream, and dill (or tarragon) together. Season. Microwave on a high setting for approximately 2 minutes—based on 650W (reduce the time for a more powerful microwave). Spoon $^{1}/_{4}$ of the mixture on top of each pile of salmon strips. Warm the tartlets through in the oven for about 10 minutes before serving. Garnish with a frond of fresh tarragon or dill.

Makes 4

HAWAIIAN TART

DOUGH:
1 recipe Basic Pie Dough (page 9) but replacing 3
  tablespoons of the flour with freshly grated
  coconut (or dried, shredded coconut)
FILLING:
1 tablespoon butter
1 medium brown onion, sliced
1-inch piece fresh ginger, peeled and grated
4 slices cooked ham, cut into thin strips
4 pineapple slices (canned or fresh)
3 large eggs
1/2 cup sour cream
freshly ground black pepper to taste
2/3 cup (2 oz) cubed buffalo mozzarella

Preheat oven to 375F (190C). Make the
dough, adding the coconut after cutting the
butter into the flour. Cover in plastic wrap
and chill for 15 minutes. Melt the butter in
a skillet and sauté the onion and ginger for
10 minutes until just browned. Transfer to a
plate lined with paper towel. Roll the dough
out to a 1/4-inch thickness and use to line an
8-inch loose-bottomed shallow tart pan.
Prick the bottom with a fork and bake blind
(without waxed paper or pie weights) for
10 minutes.

Spoon the onion mixture into the pastry
shell and add the ham so that the strips
appear ribbon-like on top of the onions. Cut
the pineapple into small chunks and add to
the tart. Blend the eggs together with the
sour cream and season. Pour over the filling
ingredients and sprinkle the mozzarella
cubes on top. Bake for 30–35 minutes until
golden and set.

Serves 4

BASKET TAMALE TART

DOUGH:
1³/₄ cups all-purpose flour
³/₄ cup fine cornmeal
³/₄ cup butter, cubed
2 medium egg yolks
1 tablespoon egg wash
FILLING:
1lb 4 oz lean coarse ground beef
1 tablespoon olive oil
1 large red onion, roughly chopped
2 red chilies, seeded and chopped
1 green chili, seeded and chopped
1 tablespoon paprika
14 oz canned tomatoes, diced
¹/₄ cup tomato paste
¹/₂ cup canned corn, drained

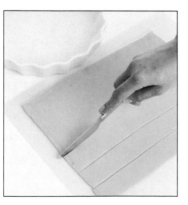

2 tablespoons chopped parsley
freshly ground black pepper to taste

Preheat the oven to 375F (190C). Place the flour, cornmeal, and butter into a food processor and blend until mixture resembles coarse breadcrumbs. Add the yolks and enough cold milk (about ¹/₂ cup) to bind the ingredients. Cover with plastic wrap and chill for 30 minutes.

Roll the dough out to a ¹/₄-inch thickness to form a 12 x 9-inch rectangle. Cut this into 1¹/₂-inch strips, lengthwise. Butter a 9-inch deep tart pan. Lay 3 strips across the bottom of the dish, leaving parallel spacing in between. "Weave" 3 strips in the opposite direction to create a "basket weave" effect. Fill in the gaps with smaller strip lengths, still following the pattern. Press joins together very lightly.

BASKET TAMALE TART

Bake the pastry shell blind for 10 minutes.
Brush the bottom with egg wash, and cook
for an additional 5 minutes.

Cook the ground beef in a large skillet for
10 minutes until browned and then transfer
to a plate lined with paper towel to absorb
the fat. Drain the remaining fat from the
skillet and wipe clean with paper towels.

Heat the oil and add the onion and chilies.
Cook for 5 minutes until softened and then
return the ground beef to the skillet. Add all
the remaining filling ingredients (but only 1
tablespoon of parsley). Simmer on a low
heat for 20 minutes. Season to taste before
spooning it into the prepared "basket."
Sprinkle with the remaining parsley and
serve.

Serves 4

FIERY MEAT FEAST TART

DOUGH:
1 recipe Basic Pie Dough (page 9)
¹/₂ cup cream cheese
FILLING:
10 oz lean beef fillet
1 tablespoon olive oil
2–3 birds eye chilies, seeded and finely chopped
1 red jalepeño chili, seeded and finely chopped
²/₃ cup roughly chopped pastrami
¹/₂ cup spicy cooked pork sausage, diced
2 large eggs
¹/₃ cup skim milk
1 tablespoon capers, roughly chopped
²/₃ cup grated Monterey Jack cheese
freshly ground black pepper to taste
6 cherry tomatoes, halved

Preheat the oven to 375F (190C). Make the dough, mixing in the cream cheese after cutting the butter into the flour. Add approximately ¹/₃ cup chilled water to the mixture to bind the ingredients together to form a soft dough. Cover with plastic wrap and chill for 15 minutes. Cut the beef into thin strips. Heat the oil in a skillet and add the beef and chilies. Cook for 5 minutes until the meat has just browned. Add the pastrami and pork sausage.

Mix the eggs, milk, capers, and cheese together. Season. Roll the dough out to a ¹/₈-inch thickness and lift into the bottom of an 8-inch loose-bottomed tart pan. Trim away any excess with a rolling pin. Brush the pastry bottom with the egg mixture. Prick lightly with a fork and bake blind for 10 minutes before adding the meat mix. Pour egg mixture over filling and top with the tomato halves. Bake for 35–40 minutes until golden brown and the filling has set.

Serves 4

CORNED BEEF FLAN

DOUGH:
1²/₃ cups all-purpose flour
¹/₄ cup each of butter and shortening
1 tablespoon freshly chopped parsley
¹/₃ cup chilled water
FILLING:
4 hash brown potato cakes, (thawed if frozen)
1 tablespoon canola oil
1 large brown onion, halved and sliced
2 garlic cloves, peeled and crushed
13 oz canned corned beef
3 large eggs
¹/₂ cup skim milk
8 basil leaves
freshly ground black pepper to taste
¹/₃ cup grated sharp cheddar cheese

Preheat the oven to 375F (190C). Place the flour, butter, and shortening into the bowl of a food processor and blend using the pulse action. Add the parsley and enough water until mixture binds together in a dough. Remove from the processor, cover in plastic wrap, and chill for 15 minutes. Cut each hash brown into 4 strips. Heat the oil in a skillet and cook the onion and garlic for about 8 minutes, over a gentle heat, until golden brown. Turn the corned beef out into a bowl and break up with a fork. Blend the eggs and milk together.

Chop the basil into thin strips and add to the bowl. Roll dough out to a ¹/₄-inch thickness and use to line a 9-inch loose-bottomed tart tin. Spoon the onions and garlic into the pastry flan and cover with the corned beef. Top with the hash brown strips, in an even pattern, and pour in the egg mixture. Season and sprinkle the cheese over the top. Bake for 40–45 minutes until golden brown and the filling has set.

Serves 6

INDEX